THE NIGHT SKY

THE NIGHT SKY

RENÉE VERONA
PARADISE'S POET

www.rarityofparadise.com
© 2017 Antonio Bommer

All rights reserved. No portion of this book may be reproduced in any form without permission from the publisher, except as permitted by U.S. copyright law
Publisher: Antonio Bommer

ISBN: 978-0-692-86829-4

Dedicated to:
A star that sits fairly adjacent to the moon

I wonder...

If we were stars would we fall together?
I wonder...How many people would wish upon us for the sake of their love?

Would our destinies be lock together then?

Could we finally stream throughout the heavens as if we were angels?
Free falling in each other's arms protected by the light illuminating from our hearts?
Maybe then we would be destined...destined to soar together above these clear skies.

I wonder...Is it because we are not stars that we suffer such cruel fates?

Our destinies will always intertwine but,
Will fate ever share in the ebb tides of our joy my love?

I wonder...If we were stars would we fall to change someone's else fate?
And if we were destined...where we destined to fall together?

RENÉE VERONA

STARFIRE

Within the fading dawn stood two twin tulips,
And upon their lips, words petal-ed with elegance held an atomic bliss that spoke of relics,
Whispering tales belonging to a void which bloomed thereof the color amethyst
Coinciding, within the evolution tied to a blank consciousness,
A big bang became this siren shedding particles of enlightenment...Thus, there it all began,

A story of two that dawned in the echoes,
Echoing ever and everlasting between two beloved conduits
Those channeling forever transmitting reincarnation, dreams, and love lasting for a lifetime

...And of a lifetime thereafter...

Nothingness personified I was, while she shined as the architect of creation,
Dancing to the silent sounds of empty space, for music was of her soul,
And I, a somber entity took pity upon my own, as I knew not those acoustic harmonies
But I knew surely of her image and of her grace...What a waste my existence would have been,
If say her embrace was never misplaced upon this lonely vastness

...Sublime, yet superficial I believe... nevertheless

A wonderment herald her creation ergo,
She wandered becoming Venus and I to follow stood as Mars
A god unto mankind, likewise she a goddess in form
How could I not adore this idol who sat ideally within my mind

The heaven's shook every time the planets aligned,
And I vibrated sighs as I glared upon her vibrant skies

However, my tremors grew fairly dim
When the tranquilities beaming from her cosmic lullabies quivered ever so benevolent
Such benevolence lost to, as well as within a nebula's gripping gauntlet
There roaming comets found a home around her aesthetics, waltzing to an enchanting gentle tune

A miracle having chaos to mimic beauty, henceforth let the chaos ensue
Thusly I awoke, as if it was all, but a dream, behold in view the royal fool

...Courting only his humor tailored to a wishful truth, then I saw you...

Queen Alexis a dreams undying proof,
Another time in eternity we found ourselves profoundly renewed

THE NIGHT SKY

While two twin tulips laid resting between your intertwining hair locks,
A being covered in petals of forget me nots was crowned with a tiara tainted a sapphire blue
Causing me to jest justly about my jesting gestures
And how flowers will always bloom envious of you

…C'est la vie vue, ma star…
It's an act simply showcasing a diminutive admiration for one as beautiful as she is acute
…Label it an unyielding virtue, that attuned…

Many moons sighted our courtship, the Montague escorting a captivating Capulet
An empress, hereby sovereign, fully extravagant, poised, together a Bellatrix far beyond elegant
Perplexed I seem, considering too often I linger amidst the confines of my own mind,
A bit mesmerized or rather overly mystified,
For angels, may sing souls into serenity, but I pray none hummed a hymn quite like hers

Fa la la…la la…la fleur de dieu

And, yes I do melt to the sounds of her voice,
So solely benign as a fifth dimensional curve strips us from this reality
My, if beauty itself had a name and a face,
So surely would it be this creature in my eyes, as infinite as time

A cattleya for my dearest Albina,
The light that beckons in the night sky, thereof the morn we became birds if only to fly
Within a paradise where two twin tulips held a fairytale that told secrets pertaining to our love,

My love, quoting ravens and those nightingales
That song a song reiterating that a queen and a fool where once planetary gods

Created from nothing, but a void be loving the pulse fire who ignited star fire within a big bang
Reincarnating through the phantasms shaping reality,
Behold heaven's sacred duality, one ebony another ivory
And with every rebirth those tulips grew all to majestic emulating our essence
Fading with the dawn, just to dawn in the twilight

Imagine if you will the ebb and flow of a quantum tides
Forever doesn't seem long enough when I am by your side
To a spirit that embodies a queen, a flower, and a star
…wait for me, the infatuated bard singing a song

One more adieu I care little to prolong, therefore come quickly my final chime
As two twin tulips wither away in this moment,
For in the next my Juliet, lies another cherished lifetime…

RENÉE VERONA

A GLIMPSE AT SOMETHING BEAUTIFUL

Imagine if you will a somewhat subtle ripple in time, a fatal glimpse at something beautiful
A wonderment that could bring envy to those blooming flowers, and to that benevolent sky
Take for a second a moment to envision a division from what we labeled as the norm
To view a beloved sight of a radiant woman that sparks the inspiration within a man's soul

Somewhere lost in that isolated drifting twilight zone I dared to be so bold
As I versified the image of a pearl like perceptional daydream
Which, pertains to one that personifies my thoughts of celestial beings

...Angels is what I mean...
An angel that for a moment alleviated my foolish iniquities,
And, who am I to deny what seems so divine
Holding this second a certain breath left fading into time

Therefore, I ask why are creatures of your caliber created by the hands of whatever god?
As it feels all to unfair to a dreamer
Who dreams only to reclaim these untamed muses cascading from this vital life of mine

An example, seeing what is beauty masking that structure belong to your enchanting face
Infused with an aura which outlines your unperishable essence and your perpetual grace...

Perhaps, I linger in this state of admiration to long
But, in this continuum where gravity became virtually a weightless commodity
It was none but you who grounded my eyes from the heavens above

...Maybe, it will be your smile that is to be forever a charm immortalized within my mind...

Slowly...claiming fully my cerebral conscious time
An impression far more gentle than a lover's kiss or a delicate lullaby
Thus, if ever the world believed it was not of significance, and the stars fell from the sky
Underneath the sun would bloom a flower unto all flowers...a goddess in her prime.

Vaguely, do I remember the night,
For my eyes have closed themselves off to the darkness.

And in the shadows of my memories
Do you stand. as the void in the depths of my bottomless heart.

You are a seed to any black thoughts
That finds themselves corrupting my empty, yet agonizing mind.

In view the star that fell from heaven during the time of a moon lit sky

THE NIGHT SKY

THE HEMLOCK LOVE

A dire sickness painted as a satin silhouette
Her dancing shadows looming among these velvet flashbacks
Therefore, fumbling frantically I have become lost
To those feeble feelings that someone else would call love…

Lily

It's nothing more than an overdose of dopamine others would say
But, the euphoria laced within goes far beyond those complex chemicals
For, the side effects that linger are almost always fatal
Thus, pour again the sweet taste of poison, which I desire

I implore

Whereas, there was a time scripted by time when I felt an emotion
One that perfectly blended chaos with peace
In order, to create something beautiful and unique
Like the way her presence shook worlds, or at least mine, making my heart weak

I remember her voice, her smile, those eyes, and more
The lore to the madness knocking at my mind's poetic door
Cradle me in your arms, my dearest Lenore
And, I will be the raven quoting this – that "I will leave you nevermore"

Nigh

Ever so the ebb and flow breathing deeply the ebb tides of my beloved's name
Such a shame, surely I can subside this pain
Wed locked within the hemlock known as love;

Oh, one more time maybe far too much
But, I will drink and if I should die – love would be the reason that I lie
…A sip to Paradise's creed her image will forever taint me,
Here's to love, and may mercury heal this foolish king

Alexis, to you…cheers to my Queen

RENÉE VERONA

QUEEN ALEXIS & THE KING OF FOOLS

Can I for a moment tell you a story…A tale that is but a whisper in our noble royal court
Herein this fable lies a fool along with a beautiful queen named Alexis
And every day the unwise comic would sing to the majestic maiden
Seeking only to enchant her heart, because that which was of his, sat only as hers

Many moons went by, thus many times did he make her smile
And day by day she became more and more of that which was thereof his undying inspiration

"My, you are quite the entertainer" her royal highness spoke so eloquently

"It's just I jest justly about being a jester to justify my jesting gesture
Towards this everlasting love I have for thee" replied the clever trickster

"I take it that you are flirting with me?" asked the queen

"I am a fiend … a night crawler gifted with the ability to amuse my muses
Nothing more my queen, I wouldn't dare to become such a fool." answered the royal jester

Then Alexis said, "Well I guess I am blessed that you are already such a fool."

"And you are a wise queen with a skillful insight to see through these verbal riddles
Which, I leave behind, while hoping with secrecy that I may one day be fit as a king so,
That this clown could escape a tragedy, which has been made
Sorely as novel displaying my emotions of longing for someone" responded the jester

…They adored each other and their bond grew ever so strong
In private they would dance together, as well as take slow walks underneath the silver moon
Their affection was innocent furthermore was it all too very, very pure

Although, life itself had a dark sense of humor
People starting questioning the queen
Slandering and making rumors and of why she was spending so much time tied to a fool
Her image and pride became thin, and what was once love became a scorned hatred

The fool was not at all as he dressed; He took notice and soon broke her gentle heart,
So, that her people would love her again as he did…meaning without question
Consequently, to the guillotines she sent him,
With a heavy heart, she was to make short a manifested joke

Therefore, in chains…bound to those rusty old shackles the jester spoke his last words saying
"I will love you forever" hysterically as the mouton blade fell
With the tears from his beloved Alexis…with tears from his beloved queen
Let the people stare at the King of fools…beheaded for what was always meant to be

THE NIGHT SKY

CHRONOMATIC

Let's consider this distorted realm akin to infinite possibilities
There, center stage lies a phantom, a fourth dimensional savant,
A charismatic void infused with concrete conscious thoughts
Solidified by a stagnate transparent plane of energy mistaken as a lawless continuum

Yet, this pendulum, which is not, but an entity everlasting to one's own personal views
Makes reality relative to those synchronizing ripples tied to a fluctuating space that
Swings ever so severely, evidently…proving thee structural evidence of an existing anomaly
A parallel perceptional universe, a paradox loosely dressed and weighted as time

Atomic, galactic, regional or otherwise
All, seemed to have their own illusionary opera actively ticking subatomic-ly aligned
Thus, in our mind's is it all simply… prospectively a notion cinematically divine
Very define, together fine and finite are these intricate workings
Individually lost to a covenant of chrono-matic crystalized quartzes labeled as our lives

An ethereal delay predating a mortified break within a diverted timeline

Therefore, spilt the resonating phases frequently converging those neutrons
To bind photonic historical electrons to a nebula like fragmented prism
Quantum-ly count the spatial virtual particles and colliding cosmic esoteric masses
Trapped within a demi-titan's hourglass, whose hope equivocal to mine
Advocates that a moment would find eternity, allowing whispers kindred to love to shine

…Everlasting…
Through the quatrains that upholds a one-sided mask that hides an ill-favored face…

What if that tantalizing trinket called time only shifted because we are perpetually traversing
Bending a petrified space coinciding said novelty stretching a falsifiable truth
With every molecule entangled to its own impending final sense entitled as a broken tempo
The inescapable…improbable…maybe my dear…but afflicted I am to think so nonetheless

A secret with an accelerated flow unfolds

Things that are truly weightless can transcend the confinements of time
Teeming Thus, what I mean to say, my love, is that when I am with you
I feel as if I am floating dimensional within a kaleidoscope of temporal golden clouds
Elevated beyond this anticipate lie…as your love defies a wrath smiting from evanescent gods

Or at least…or at least this is what I chose to believe,
For, the only imminent ties I will never deny are constructed fully by the faith I have in you
Everything else is just gears glitch-ing, twitching like those beloved stars in the night sky

RENÉE VERONA

BESAME MUCHO

Always now do I find myself stargazing at this night sky
Which, floods my eyes with the sight of celestial space particles
And in an everlasting time, I forever seem to be lost to a collapsing gravitational cloud
That breeds with such matter that its ambiance is beyond interstellar and it glows vibrantly so

As it poses to be
A fundamental phenomenal paradox to my greatest sins and my lingering woes
Thereby, Kiss me generously underneath these engraved ice halos
As pulsating variables guide cosmic planetary cycles to align with geometric planetary cocoons

Attracting ionized molecules for a fool
To fall in love while glaring deeply into the Galilean moons
For, it would be as if Apollo and Calisto violently infused

To create tectonic tyranny among distorted known galaxies
Where they all danced in spirals to the sounds of Andromeda's enduring Newtonian tune
One eclipse pass noon upon an ecliptic plane I saw pulse fire in a majestic blue

You swiftly flew as an ultra violet symmetrical outline with a radiating helix
Causing magnetic disturbances, dismantling a king from his throne, thus I threw
Useless rhetoric to a beautiful Bellatrix who
Emits solar flares while summoning black holes to consume Utopia's light and Europa's view

The only photonic deity that should ever exist in my world is to be you

Therefore, what equates from the critical velocity of this brief evolution is a simple wish
Through, the written binary that forms focal ratios trailing along the latitude equating to zero
Which, is just another intergalactic variation of the word infinity…Steganography,
Bound to quantum physics teeming slightly towards the realm of astrophysics

But, if I must simplify these emotions guarded by an astral armada of nebula like citadels
I would simply put it like this… with these words you once whispered in a song to me
Besame Mucho my dear…Besame Mucho…endlessly and without fear

THE NIGHT SKY

FLEUR DE LIS

Magnify the magnitude of this modified motif – a masterpiece posed in motion
Manipulating my vision, thus be stilling my eyes upon her image
A beauty that in the wake of, even Aphrodite became a falsified specter to

So, who am I to deny my own eyes the joys of such a glorious sight?

Thereby, hear the sounds
That are composed from the angel's echoing whispers blooming within thy ears
And embrace that affectionate fixation justifying a divine passion coded a delicate wonder
Shaping the heaven's skies
To match the priceless pearls portrayed as the pupils within her photonic eyes

Benign

No man can deny the rapid rhythm contorting the core that sits within his own chest
Therefore, Infatuation vindicating the inclination of benevolence is said to manifest…

Look at her the eclipse eclipsing his every thought; As she bends the night sky around her light
The virtues tied to admiration will always cascade from that mesmerizing, ethereal moon
Nerve impulses attune to the neurons flooding my cerebellum eagerly looms
When I long to stare at that midnight satellite…

My, this belle will forever be my muse within the twilight
A construct curving an ocean of poetry, proficiently, potent with a paralyzing personality
Thee enchanting Gorgona making a stone fool to these ill prepared romantic souls of man

Thus, I stand

In awe towards this hypnotizing majestic creature simply labeled as a woman
Particularly, this woman that embodies the effervescent essence coin as a fleur de lis
And like lilies, does she not bloom vibrantly, also when that noble sun is vigorously shining
Hence, the bashful smile infesting my lips, graceful while adorned to her presence

Now, take gemstones of every kind…gold that once stained the hands of kings
Platinum plated pieces laced with silver fragments falling from those metallic meteorites
Mistaken as comets carrying my beloved wish to dream again and throw it all away

The inspirational conundrum lies within a falsifiable lie, the key to her magnetic perfection

RENÉE VERONA

LIKE LILIES

Tremble at the gentle sounds of turmoil
That plays from the beating melody of your broken heart
Stand in the winter's wind to embrace the lingering chill
Of that which was left by the frozen soul of a lost lover

As the moon eclipses our dearly departed promises
The sun sets with our beloved dreams

Together... yet alone
Do these shadows of sadness fulfill these lonesome tears, and in the night
Do we stare deeply into the memoirs of our eluding past?
Hoping to hold onto desperately... those fleeting memories of joy

But a flower no matter how beautiful it maybe
Can never reclaim a petal once lost

So, towards the shattered pieces, that we had once deemed as paradise,
Do we walk with sorrow
Along praying for the whispers of that misplaced love to bloom anew

Though time proves to be a well-known cruel god
Therefore, in time, like lilies, do those moments wither and die
Thus, all that is left is a reminiscing void
Cursed with the sinister will of a shallow faith that one may love again

Weary smiles befall the fool
Foolish enough to lose themselves to that kind of madness...Weary fools... such as I

It seems that stars that fall from the night sky
Leaves an imprint within the mind of those that watches
Such as an angel that falls from grace
That burning sight intensifies as a fading holy trail of your glory lingers in the heavens

It's sad, for with my hands I was unable to prevent a god given fate
But even though you fell as I failed
You found a way to gracefully preserve your beauty

To the lost star that struck my heart

The sky mimics my tears with its raindrops
And it's funny, because I know it's only God mocking me
But there is no resentment or animosity I only blame this pain that I bear
On the weakness of my own naive adolescence

THE NIGHT SKY

A BEAUTIFUL DREAM

Pulsating blood vessels illuminates the broken biometrics tied to those primordial energies
That replicated a moon-lit cosmic view of an atmosphere inspired by heaven's wonders
Therefore, peel back sights belonging to dismay and sit with me for a while,
While Ave Maria sings songs, hymns, and poetry to the world and to her elevated god

Watch as these mechanics operating under the chaotic order of the universe
Bridge together subatomic uncertainties with these planetary anomalies
Thus, making reality remarkable as we reminisce so timelessly about future tidings
For lost within the echoes of Chronos we shall become as deity akin to eternal entities

Beings transcending beyond this moment and this fading hour that claims our passionate souls
Those sanctified in hieroglyphic citadels covered in cryptographic golden chromosomes

However, take now this white robe and purify those old forsaken sins you no longer hold
So, you may behold this tranquility which is calling us closer to a vivified emerald hue
That covers a soft and gentle meadow, as beautiful as the halo that has been crowned upon you

You…My Regina… My star fire which proliferates life among this void
One who sleeps in my heart very dearly
Manifesting a virtuous nebula relevant to the rippling tides pertaining to my joy, hence
Principio tailored towards our destino thee omega that is only found in a benevolent Paradiso

…Ergo…

From those dimensional phases fluctuating the densities dancing along the edges of black holes
Our story awaits through the ages to be foretold as atoms split and cells divide
Through the eons where mortals become more so divine, relinquish that foolish human pride
Intertwined we are you and I…quantified for lifetimes and thereafter… and after for lifetimes

(Some beautiful dreams are perpetual nightmares beloved and cherished by others, and sometimes I wander in these daunting phantasms looking for answers to why I lost what was so beautiful to me. Why I am so weak and how can I become more… and Love more… to elevate to a point to where I simply understand. You see the pain of love doesn't bother me nor do these sleepless nights concern me; Although my torment resides only in the chambers of my own ignorance… So, let me daydream a little longer, my love, before I will move on…Before I let go…and before I wake up and accept this reality that you are not there for me anymore.)

RENÉE VERONA

BLUE

In favor of my last breath I will speak the word indigo
Whereas, peerless is the sight of blue
Among the ocean and among the sky that rains down sapphire fragile tears

Applauded the encore belonging to a returning season of the royal hue…

As the wind carries away our burdens and our woes dire intensity
Slowly, my cerulean princess dance along this river with me
Then gently sing to me vivified viridian vocals vindicating my lust for thee…

Hymns once tailored to an imperial degree

For, two times two spirits knew love to be painted teal underneath an iris moon
Therefore, with a timely finesse that held a tint dye celeste
Midnight daisies bloomed a perfect image and said image t'was you

Tranquil in the mind I have become violet as our wavelengths intertwine
Thus, thine art mine…so thy heart will be immortalized
Forever and ever beyond that which is a never-ending time…

…Benign, Flashback to a non-photonic view…

Where the electrical sparks struck that deep indigo sky
Having electromagnetic gems encrust the heavens with those, sapphire like lies
And peerless to the sight of navy fireflies
A celestial angel would be the last and only image I see before I die

Because, it was you the perfect image that painted this encore a cloudy violet hue
Thereby, beneath that moon gripping the tides of this ocean
A princess to love will dance immortal with the color…

THE NIGHT SKY

CATTLEYA

Somber shadows often see a color shade which tends to cover a garden rose
But all too often, do we overlook these flowers themselves; it's our vile vanity I suppose
Thus, it seems those maybe the eerie thoughts tailored for assassin,
One who is becoming frigid and cold
So, listen for a moment, as in a moment the composition of my will shall be composed

…Woes in the twilight hours found vividly exposed…

Throughout the night my covenant friend edged of sharp steel knew only a murderous intent
While the moon sat in the sky as our guide, with a silent chill as a comforting hand fairly present
Onward we raced ever so episodically towards a smell that intoxicated the air with iron
Fulfilling an unyielding blood-lust we shared; surely a quantum tide accelerating particles of fire

Strange it felt, that this bond I had with an onslaught never appeared to be foreign or shameful
I delighted in the wake of was to be a swift and frequent culling
As my blade belonged to the kingdom's king, and I more than honored obeyed his crown
Furthermore, was I proud, therefore any foe unto my lord, a future corpse, my oath and vow

Still, fading chimes; hence beautiful are these ebbing thymes and the parallel decaying time

I find a bit lost I am, while and when staring at particular petals depicted as indigo
Let me show you Fibonacci's greatest secret among a cryptic cosmos
Observe faint filled whispers set between the delicate seconds of my dying ethos

…For therein lays her sweet, gentle name…

Cattleya, a flora she pointed ever so fondly at during a summer's midday
Ergo, Astray I presumed myself I would say
When I became seduced by the virtues of this woman's smile and of her imperial eyes
Forever taken by her… "Lovely are they not," she asked… "Enchanting," I replied
Then, thusly I plucked the soft vine's defenseless stem…A gift for one so very benign within

"Why rush something that is inevitable" she cried
Just as I watched as tears flooded from her now un-tranquil mind
"Death comes for everything" she sighed "All life is precious for life's fate is to die"
Naïve I thought as I left with no returning gestures or any talented goodbyes

…Some men are evil and are blessed with a quick demise…

Feel that ominous breeze corrupting the midnight, caressing thy face, echoing tales of the moonlight
You killed my father and brother a boy screamed as I beheld a cattleya blooming in the night
Fight we did, however I could only see Cattleya's eyes;
Distracted by the thoughts that I was the evil one in this boy's life

…My assassin's pride made me so blind…

RENÉE VERONA

The clashing duel raged on,
And honestly I wanted to spare this child if only to protect her essence for while
Forfeiting guile and reckless I became as the boy stumble towards that prolific flower,
A grand effort I made to push him away,

Yet, therein that moment my grim dismay, for I rushed directly into his vengeful blade

Prospectively, there laid a change in a killer's heart that slowly became more concave
A bit of wisdom at my grave... divine "All life is precious" my atoning last line
So fondly I pointed at that beloved flower reflecting upon my sinful crimes
Lovely are they not Cattleya asked me once
As enchanting as a garden's rose was my final un-forsaken but dimming thoughts

(In that moment I understood what precious life truly was... Thank you my unspoken love.)

The stars would not have fallen if it wasn't for her
Stardust wouldn't have rain throughout the cosmos if she did not appear

But now I am surrounded by a storm of a glisten wonder
That is eroding the eradicated land that I stand upon...

It seems as if fate aligned our worlds
So, that heaven could see an everlasting tempest bury itself within my essence
And to my discomfort It has;

Yet, I do not frown upon this aspects of life of which was held by a celestial goddess
One who scared the night sky just so that I could know beauty
In a baron earth I thought was ignorant to this characteristic

I simply see it as an agonizing gift that she left me with
A daunting promise of remembrance
As well as a piece of paradise that was created by God
With the purpose of intertwining our noble restless souls

THE NIGHT SKY

-FA LA LA

Hold me one more time my love
I am fading into an absent state of mind
Falling from this abstract, ambient dream painted thereof peace an isolated hue

Strange, I cannot bring myself to pluck flower petals from these flowers
For, in time like I, will they wither in die
So, I empathize…sympathizing to the point of vanity
Caring in a way that may allow them to have but a few more moments to sing

With those vibrant colors, which add a verity of tones to this dying world…I mean
It seems we tend to rush that which is meant to be
Death looms, love is forever, and our consciousness fiends for them to sets us free

Fa la la…la la…la fleur de dieu (The Flower of God)
The misplaced lullaby that wanders in my lost corrupted mind

Kiss me one more time my love
As I am aging, decaying, and declining to see the hope in tomorrow
Yet, your lips…the gentle curves of your rejuvenating lips
And their passionate touch revitalizes my faith

In that your beautiful face, will be there when I awake within that un-promised morning
Just like those flower petals I felt for, took pity on and dreamt about
Thereby, if by the grace of God may you be my flower to which I could care for

Thus, within these fleeting moments tied to time I would paint pictures dedicated to you
Lacing emptying canvases with a sheen that mimics your vibrant esoteric glow
Having your image to be the reason my quill floods a page with nonstop poetry

All to make something like your essence everlasting
As if you were to corrupted the mind of God
As this lullaby has mine…Fa la la…la la…la fleur de dieu a perpetual ambient hue

RENÉE VERONA

THINGS EVERLASTING

Standing indefinite in this parallel perception inverted for a moment
Lies a fragile memory acting as a paradigm prioritizing an unforgettable paradox
Which, is infinitely a sentiment of equilibrium innately caressing my cerebellum...
But, whatever may come of my fragmented mind an angelic notion will transcend time

One harboring the attributes of things everlasting, compelling these vital shadows of mine
Yet, causing me to become disoriented for as I loved, I also lost her love with my pride
Thus, astray I sway between dreams and actually...reality and illusion; Delusion
The vanity of my sanity fell towards a boundless retribution tied this broken world

As occasionally I spoke to her without her being here
And when life granted fatigue we laid together...However,
I awoke only to a sense of despair for honestly she was never there
Unfortunately, I can no longer find that draw line which parts the factual and the fable...

(...Yes, my love I will see you soon ...Yes, my dear I will love you forever as I promised...)

Forgive me, I seem to be slipping once again
I would guess that I am effected heavily by these enchanting emotion,
And daydreams quoting her questions regarding my proclaimed unforsaken vows
So, allow me this clemency
As I indulge myself with images belonging to the past or to those mistaken present novelties

Also, let me look foolishly at this angel that I remember from a time ago
Watch as I whisper at the wind, and with the wind; for I truly believe she is right beside me
More so, give me the chance to feel somewhat sensible
Even if, this opportunity that I reach so frantically for fades in the end as she does

Because, what was became all to lucid as those stars crossed the night sky
Still, nocturnal to it all, I blindly walk only where my heart echoes, thereby
Tragedy may hope to follow and I may display simply a sad portfolio...nonetheless
In spite, of this...as deranged as I know I am, I will know that some things are in fact made real

...Like these flashbacks that keep reoccurring...

(Man: If I follow
– Woman (whispering): Then you will lead
Man: And, I will you love forever
– Woman (whispering): And ever it seems.)

Like these visions of paradise
In my sub-consciousness always painted as a beautiful portrait unyielding and perpetually rare

THE NIGHT SKY

ENCHANTÉE

Burning molecules ionizing, so much so,
That a godlike light labeled as plasma forms
And lighting strikes from the hands of a God reaching sadly only a stone's throw
Inscribe among these fragmented parchments heaven's broken tempo

Do I dare face the agony tied to a lonely tomorrow alone?

Who knows what off brand chemistry will infest the air
Hence, I ask myself is this the strength that I claim to bare

Enduring a self-inflected pain that is slowly eradicating my heart
Lying to myself saying "the marrow shall be bejeweled with brightness"
Believing that the steps I take are bring me closer to an angelic star
Deluded views of paradise now seen as sacred scars

For, the more I reach, the more la lumiere' pulls away

Because, always has sun traversed across that open-ended sky therefore,
Perceptional-ly the actuality of my efforts has, in reality, been just a wasted stand still
The generosity belonging to a vivified vanity shares it's undying will…

…Such laboring hope can be such a trifling and terrible thing…

But, I can stare deeply into this everlasting frigid void for an eternity
Although, my fragile grip on time would certainly be consumed
And, I may forever become lost to these memories
Which, I had once for a life…that I had once lived; An existence never to be forgotten

Forbore a dream est…a la vie…or…est a la mort…
A riddle captivated by hamlet, thereby me too I suppose
I long simply as a man missing a part of his infatuated soul thus,
Enchantée am I via my own crippling woes; imposed upon by this enchanting delicate rose

Nevertheless…C'est la vie, mes amies…
…Yet, I must say, oh what a rose in my life she was…

RENÉE VERONA

A RUBY COLORED SAPPHIRE

Vandalize the vivid voices vanishing with those conceded diamonds
Painted benign beyond that flawless Persian moon
That which was once scorn by the fire trapped within her eyes
And unto her eyes reigned the sun thus of the sun am I forever tied

Blanket her sleeping soul with amber embers that dance upon the tiger lilies lips
So, that I may show you a creature that stands as a nova among a nebula of stars

Moreover, tell me, is it really, so bad to die for something as simple as a kiss
What if that kiss ignited a cosmic flame that echoed for light-years and lifetimes?
Allowing space to shift into that of time
Making such a moment a converted love and love a reality proclaimed as mine

My, would the angels sing...Oh, would the heavens rejoice...

Along this void inked with a hue stained by these ruby colored sapphires
Much like those bejeweled perceptional petals instilled as the irises of her eyes
Akin to the lucid lights illumining this alluring looming dream

Therefore, photonic liquid pearls are set to ionize the sky
In order, to spark a notion that will carry her essence across the stratosphere
Bring heat to the atmosphere thereby warming my cold dying dire soul
Ergo, my love shall be known as fire's Calypso

Hence, Lo and behold a goddess reanimated from brimstone

...And in her benevolent eyes a soul burns so pure...
...Of her grace embers scorn the moon with a crimson view...
Can you imagine the enchanting inferno that lies upon her delicate lips?
Can you see why a man like me would die for such a simple kiss

Set ablaze unto my heart Sunna – While summer sunsets vandalized my vivid sight
Then white flames will melt man's diamonds into heaven's gold
And to this world your presence shall be eternally known

THE NIGHT SKY

LA VIE EN ROSE

Often I find myself walking with a gallery of forgotten memories looming within my mind
Even so I find it strange, that these past impressions do not seem to bother me in the slightest
However, they have always forced me to reminisce greatly about a certain beauty
A vixen that scorned my heart,
Whom of which, given her troublesome ways, I fell madly in love with

And, for her smile that bloom as beautiful as any petal belonging to a rose that colored itself pink

Now, during a summer's dream…let's say on a Sunday, sunbeams would softly shine upon her skin
While a midday breeze tended to dance with her sundress,
And I feeling sunny would idolize such a star
Through the hours of a wakeful sunrise until a somber sunset, therefore
Repeatedly would she notice me sun-gazing at the brilliancy of her incandescent sheering light

What was to fear,
I wondered, if love was forever so bright and roses bloomed a color perpetually pink

Oh, but life can bear excessively an element of cruelty at times, and one can lose such days
Although, never has my heart attempted to waver,
Thus, I guess, this may be why I daydream daily of her still

Perhaps,
My soul has been left burning because her essence, found evermore yearning for her benevolence
…My, what a presence…

Thus, be honest and frankly express an unfulfilled answer unto me
Would you ever think
A man could come to become lost, via the contemplations of his missing affections?
Say surely, I am not alone conveying these beloved sinful and, yet alluring complications
Trudging through, about, and amidst the broken shards unveiling, a lovely recollection

Kissing with the white moon's obsession
Perfectly placed herein the night sky's reflection, thee mimicking projection of her magnanimity
Giving generously unto my world a hope in serendipity, made exquisitely for these gloomy tides
Forevermore, tied charmingly to her form,
Made vividly passionate by the sun-fire inked of her splendor

Dearest amour, did you ever know that garden roses can bloom a color as pretty, as pink

And that my life seems as such when I think of you dressed in a royal mink
If only I could hold your hand in this modern time, when lovers dine with wine
Staring into each other's eyes under the moonlight speaking simply primitive sighs, benign
Would it all be as they frequently sing, that of a moment blissfully known as … "La Vie En Rose"

RENÉE VERONA

Anyhow, day by day I sit in this Eden that I stroll forsakenly to, as to wait for the first sight of roses

For who, but who knows the next shade of color that they may share
Pink, red, yellow or perchance even a navy blue
Whatever the shade may it be, may it always remind me of you

What if I gave up heaven to hold onto the stars
Would I burn like the inferno foolish ambitions that I carry
For maybe the stars are just like flowers with thorns
Beautiful, yet…they only wish to be admired from afar

Or perhaps they hope to find someone who wouldn't mind holding on to them
Even if they bare spikes of agony along their frail, fragile stems

…Whatever the case

Underneath the night sky I wait to give a flower to a lone lost star
As my hands bleed from my tightly griped hold around a flower's stem

A fool for the stars I know I am
But the pain I carry doesn't hurt so bad
Beauty holds and of that which I wish to hold
Elevates me beyond what is known to some as a mortal torment

So, let me burn with the sight of the stars
That to me is a vision of my own personal heaven

THE NIGHT SKY

A VAGUE ENCORE

Encore for the whimsical ranting thoughts
Hysterically vindicating the gallows
As red ink spills across the envious emerald eyes
Fooled to shut in fear – at the sounds belonging to an almighty scream

A relentless scream that hails its own encore
Reanimating pain and the paths in which lay throughout the universe
Known as cosmic dreaming – tip toeing in my dreams

Laced with the thorns clipped from a rose's stems
Together held parallel to the bittersweet images
Swimming along the fading memories colliding my lost beloved with a cluster of stars

…Heavenly it seems

Yet, these nocturnal visions make no sense I'm afraid
They speak to me though it's abstract and of their own language
…A pulsing whisper…very lovely, but all to faint and vague to comprehend at times

Much like a lifetime compared to an eternity
Or a single note embedded within a symphony revered as a masterpiece
A star among many I suppose, but none far too radiant enough to match her face

…Forgive me,
Where is the correlation, perhaps my mind is scattered?
Subconsciously riddled with flashbacks and tender moments that I have tried to forget

Therefore, in my dreams beside those relentless thoughts
An encore plays… a masterpiece of my lifetime whispering abstract visions
So, heavenly that my lost beloved image may remain that of a thorn less rose

…And with such a rose…How could I ever forget….

RENÉE VERONA

CONVOLUTED

An iconic state of confusion
Is slowly cultivating itself into my already convoluted mind
It's like I'm slipping further and further away… towards a tainted twilight
Which has been immensely riddled with particle eclipses and paranormal skies

Once more would I like to hear the talented goodbyes
That screams from the ongoing raging sunset
As it agonizes over its own looming demise

The lonesome soul forever tied to a personified wasteful vanity
A vampiric like lust held by a dense dark destiny thus gravity
To think that light would even shine in this black pearl of life that is mine

…Hysterical, and together all to horrifying to comprehend
But, beautiful nonetheless

Akin to the notion of a raving senseless composer
Slamming his fingertips upon the archaic piano's broken keys
Hoping for the world to understand the melody
That would thrive from the chaos of his overbearing heart

The simpleton left daring… always daring for an everlasting encore

How delusional can one man be
However, what is a man without his dreams
Can you now see why I am so uncertain about my own sanity?
As I watch this setting sun burn with its first and last dying cry

I only wish I could trap this sight within my eyes
To let this view, remain throughout the night
Perhaps then my soulless stare would gleam with wonder
Allowing me to look clearly beyond this obscure turmoil that lies

A clouded magic vindicated, thus I ask who dares to dream otherwise

THE NIGHT SKY

BELLISSIMO

"Who knew that beauty itself could be infatuated by your cosmic eyes."

Whispered I unto Aphrodite as she became the ebb and flow of my affection
That was tied forever unto the intoxicating impression of a noble essence
Thus, forever was I to find myself lost to a notion found fragmented by time
A sentiment so closely refined held divinity to entwined a purity that bloomed from a lilium's lips

Still, of your lips that fornicates with a tantalizing bliss, my beloved Aphrodite, I stand convinced
That not even arrows of Eros could even be as captivating as your persuasive kiss…thus wonderment
And words cascading from my heart as I persisted, to make everlasting what was already heaven sent
Therefore, lucid I stared into a stone made of amethyst hoping to compare your elegance

For all to compelling was this Venus who along life's dreaded riviere danced in an enchanting volvre,
But, there in a majestic moment I awoke from an elevated sense of providence

Por favor mi amor, do not leave me again

Because, for a time now I have found myself drowning within a liquid profane
Hoping to look pass this world were in my eyes shades of shame dance with flames
Which burns ever so passionately like these narcotics that tend ease this revolving pain
A heavy heart to weight furthermore, I remain a tattered fiend tied to a beloved Novocain

As crystals create a beautiful sight of poison to mesmerize those inebriated membranes
That falls in love with a stimulant so vain,
I, However, wish for more only to hold you, my bella, a bit longer before I say a grim nevermore

A spirit so poor…The weakness and tears of a man hidden within sedatives and cocaine…

Likely among this inferno a vision of my Aphrodite, the planetary goddess to whom of which I miss
Hold me throughout the night as the fluid acid fulfills this lingering emptiness; A perfect madness…
Who knew that beauty itself could be infatuated by your cosmic eyes
Whispered I unto Aphrodite,
As I knew life no more, yet upon my heart burned my lover's tattooed lore

Which displayed an eternal sun traversing across a moonless night sky,
Bellissimo, I will say was this life of mine and of the moments that we often shared,
My Aphrodite,
Heaven is a perceptional thing, and you unto me, was the perception of heaven's dreams

RENÉE VERONA

TO MARVEL AT A DREAM

I marvel at the universal scale
Plated empty the vastness of space and how fragile it all really...is
The planets and suns...moons and of course the stars
All dancing on these subatomic quivering quantum strings

Those that are made to be incomprehensible to the common man
For the multitude of atoms that make up this galaxy and my body
Seems to fall at a sight beaming with particles
Playing the sweet melody which sings an ongoing encore vividly versifying the word

... Fibonacci...Fibonacci is the name, although to what means...

Many times, have I counted these seconds that refuse to end
Furthermore, have I countless-ly written these words paying homage to the sky
Yet, only in this life have I been denied the secrets to that procedural heaven

At least... at least that is what I can come to remember but, perhaps it's all just lies

Therefore, sleep a while longer in your ignorance
Enjoy the bliss of not knowing what is unknown
Leave my riddles as they are, and avoid the void for some time; maybe even a lifetime
To take hold of a gift mistaken as a common commodity among commoners

As higher dimensions dressed in platinum to praise a higher conscious being

In your heart purity still lies true and bold
In your soul, the rarity of paradise is gold
Thereby in this world is a virtual dream
So, alone in that realm is this perception that you call reality and...

And, I marvel at your creation... I marvel at the scale of what it all came to be

THE NIGHT SKY

A DIVINE GYPSY MOON

Look at these unbroken tides that flood the ocean blue
And the gentle waves that sit upon the fading horizon
Watch as they ellipse at sight of your beauty
While reflecting the elegant curves of your tender lips

You see,
Onto the world you are untouched
For the seven seas, have conveyed your will
And at a glance you are the moon itself; walking in human form

Yet, what lies within the crux of this lunar light
Is the essence of a soul marked gypsy
That could travel amidst the string of my poetic heart

Thus, evermore forevermore
And furthermore, that which is all to divine

Therefore, any man foolish enough to look pass
The sacred sights of your angelic eyes
Should drown in the depths of their own misguided perception
While remaining as such until the end of time

However, I find it inconceivable for a person to be so daft

Nonetheless, I believe I have become senseless
To the glimpses of your thunder
Moreover, awe-struck by the ways of your untamed nature

That which belongs to a ruthless flower
With a seductiveness that knows no mercy
And as I stare relentlessly at this eclipsing sunset
I now stand as a fatal victim of passion

So, along these shores do I walk; Together do I drift among this coast
In astonishment for the majestic deluge
That has been captivated by the ripples that cast your image of wonder

The beloved gift of heaven that awaits in my eyes as utopia...

RENÉE VERONA

THE MOON DRESSED IN WHITE

Red wine for the moon dressed in white
And for the majestic fowls that were not black scorn ravens
But, that of divine doves fooled by the first sight of their own shadows

The birds of paradise
Which harbors over the edges of my fragile life
As if they were the angels of death waiting to claim my soul

Therefore, when I look up to heaven and see their feathers slipping from the sky
I image a volver of forsaken spirits dancing in the sun
Intertwining forever in the roots of heaven's discord
But always reaching for the doors of their own salvation

A translation similar, to the fallen puzzle pieces that were once etched in stone
There only to engrave a crucified parallel premonition
Perceiving vivified visual visions peerless to a decaying world

Thus, having time stand in the ruins belonging to those
Which have deemed themselves as intellects
With a vine of dissolution found wanting within the holy halls of judgement
As roses bloom beneath the footsteps of a sacred virgin
Lost hymns of three kings and of seven stars shall revive a dying Lazarus

The biblical shell of light that lingers upon my window…

Although, some would say part take of the devil's fruit
Because the peach is so much sweeter
Yet, my eyes have been fixated towards those moon-lit humbling clouds

…A trifling thing I suppose…

THE NIGHT SKY

ALBINA & THE BIRDS OF PARADISE

Somewhere within my cerebral cortex
Lies a lobotomized lullaby that lingers like a foul, frantic phantom
Echoing more as gentle fowls parade the open-ended sky

Listen carefully... its beautifully tormenting

Having nightingales sing memories of this known belle
Who I might add, absent of effort, caused my cerebellum to malfunction
For in a moment I fell, and nevermore it felt, that I was to fly without her

Yet the story goes, those ravens tend to know, more than this old broken crow

As in a time we glided as two doves intertwined
A picture in some eyes eternally benign, thus divine
The heliocentric couple crippled by a gap in time
Although, we had hope and a love that still makes me sigh

Reminiscent... is the lamented cardinal coded passion....

Therefore, if ever such a thing was restored
It would breathe joy onto paradise, as well as to the heavens above
Seeing as how she that gives happiness is your name, and the fault was surely mine to claim

So, Swallows feather the sparrow swift as it makes a winged descent...
The avian aerial flock majestic together aesthetic in the art of soaring beyond that horizon
Graceful you all shamelessly seem... just like her...Elegant, just like my Albina shall forever be

RENÉE VERONA

ALBINA & THE BIRDS OF PARADISE II

Within the blight of this inexplicable darkness of mine lies a spark that exhilarates every cell
Vicariously vindicating those beloved memories, I have for and of you
And, although our time together seems very disproportionate the moments we share
Only compare to that of a volvre, as we tend to dance so elegantly upon a silver sighted moon

One covered ever so delicately by the white sands
Belonging to the stardust that rains from the heavens, and from your perfect dovelike essence
Which, is something all too vigilant,
Flying absolutely, eloquently with subtle sublime virtues illuminating your avian eyes

Those that move emotionally that same enchanting, vivified moon
Allowing the ebb tides attributed to the sky to flood this heart that I attempt to deny
The core crux embedded onto my soul seemingly only there to bleed for you

A swan blessed and embodied by the stars themselves
That leads me believe you were Icarus's final view

...Thus, hopeful mines too, if fate was ever to be so kind...A tale this time

Picture a white raven migrating optimally within this illogical mind seeking always Albina the divine
Imagine his talons gripping tightly a magical locket brimming with her laughter and her smile
Preventing his tears as nevermore, never utters from the profound beak of his profane lips
When he eclipses the moon merely to admire her and the valor of her wonderment

You see...

Nightingales still sing those sacred lullabies, along with this I still stand as an old crow
Foolish to what may be regarded as perilous, but perhaps I do not care
Forevermore is what I remember quoting, forevermore was my liberating vow unto you

A promise that shall know not its own fatality,
A promise made to the stars and to a canary such as you
Look beyond that horizon;
Pass those gentle nimbus clouds, paradise sits abundant...paradise sits anew

THE NIGHT SKY

FATHER TIME – SECONDS ECHO SHORT

It's been sometime since I spoke of the rain and of the dark clouds that scream with thunder
Too long has it been for me as I watch lightning bolts illuminate the sky on this night
Are the winds high I wonder? Are they perhaps a bit chilling and cold… yes, it would seem
Such a storm during this hour of gloom is a blessing I would think

Give me thy ear as I whisper to you the ecstasy of my looming sadness

Frail and faint I have become, fragile and deprived of my strength shall my last hours be
Composing this dead man's sigh as I await my final slumber within a deathbed promising liberty
Loneliness has agreed to keep me company as we patiently anticipate his grim colleague
Although, I hope he will take his time, so I may finish lending my voice unto thee

[Several *coughs*]

Forgive me, as stated before I am weak and my next minute could mean my fatality

Nevertheless, I will speak…Now, reckless in my youth I was bold, wild as well was I free
I fell in love with the stars together with all things masked by heaven's beauty
I heard angels sing lullabies and hymns to try and give the world some sort of peace
Still, chaos reigned, but the uncertainties never really, bothered me

cough

However, there was this woman… this creature that challenged my improvident way of thinking
Fallacious she could be periodically and out right cruel if she chose to be
Nonetheless, my affection for her grew,
Thus, I began to worry of her well-being if she was not beside me

Crazy I thought I was…
Surely I was sick, because why would anyone crave "love" this potent disease
Seconds echo short though much like our time shared was compared to this approaching eternity

I speak of her now because as I die her face is the only face I see
The storm has faded from my eyes… it's just in my heart I can still hear thunder and the raging seas
A somber moment filled with the light of my beloved, what joy God has given a misguided fiend
Sweet reaper you are merciful to allow me this sight as thy black velvet cloak comforts me

Do not perish not knowing the sacred oath of love my son, to do so is one of life's greatest tragedies

(It's all relative… Love, Time…and how we perceive eternity.)

RENÉE VERONA

THE STRINGS OF MISERY

Here I am again at this door… This accursed door that only bare markings of vanity
It leads to nowhere, but if open my madness pours out, and I am left dreaming
Clinging hopelessly onto these nightmares screaming within me

Today of all day a white fowl defiled the sky allowing me to be lost in its wonder
Thus, I forfeited my consciousness to the past thoughts of an angel that haunted me ever so
Logically, she was the reason why I carried these somewhat heavy, but insignificant woes
That calibrated this delirium
Which drifted with a fifth dimensional curve into my cerebral twilight zone

Imagine if you will the compulsive pulsing fluctuation of realty
An illusion acute in form, yet indignant to the possibilities belonging to love
Many times, have I dared to endure the siphoning sight threading my insanity
Causing me to remain as he who is forever strangled by these bejeweled obscurities

The rarity of paradise trailing vividly due to a sinner's iniquities
I would call it all simply bigotry
Seamlessly, she whispered I tend to always miss understand the formalities of the word we
A selfish man I guess I was made out to be,
But, if I was anything other than myself would she have ever loved me…Perhaps

Although, therein lies our affection's fatal complexity…

Thee overlapping fear tied to tomorrows that echo with yesterday's fading beauty
Still, for some purpose this impression is everlasting, captivating with a compelling agony

I ask
Wherefore are these notions that brim from the wings of those elegant, immaculate doves
Whose benevolent presence can send a man back into an isolated primal state
One that seems to be fulfilled with the euphoria of his own self-induced torment

Tell me, a story that varies in virtue as well as validity
As I lose my self to these precise memories
Painted as something so beloved, something all to unforgettable for a shameful soul like me
To know of her love, nothing ever came close to being so sweet

…Therefore, this requiem plays on the frantic strings tainted deeply with my misery…

THE NIGHT SKY

HAZEL EYES

Frightful flickering photonic particles are set to disguise the sky
And of the satellite that wanes my madness
There lies thirteen silver pieces priced to cure that madness
Beaming a nocturnal sunlight off your radiant skin

That has been dipped in gold thus rightfully so carefully encrusted with nightly diamonds

Therefore, treasure the rarity of a lustful moment that could be as pure as love
To create said entity not of the morn but of eve
And beneath thy rib shall you know God with every atom of your passionate being
Possibly, for the chance to experience something that is everlasting

Much like a muse tied to the echoing shadows that linger
Which breathe softly words sighing a past lover's name

An anomaly to impose, I suppose ...

But, perhaps it is all a part of some cosmic plan – leading us back towards a forgotten Eden
That has been defiled by the knowledge pertaining to our own ignorance and shame
Still, able are we to be lost in such a magnitude teeming with desire

...Slowly cascading this infatuation...
The benevolent intoxication, which may only lay claim
To the invigorating taste stimulating her tempting... sweet... tantalizing lips

Thus, behind your hazel eyes I saw what could have been forever
As with a kiss I forfeited my feelings, thereby making my heart yours for the taking
However today fading....

My soul now dawdles in the memories standing as those revered so lonesome, yet benign

RENÉE VERONA

THE ESSENCE OF A STAR ONCE LOVED

You know there is this echoing whisper
That dances around my ears every time I look up at the stars
It's the wind reciting my name but with your voice
And I am haunted by your smile, our laughter, and those moments of sweet joy

Therefore, nocturnally do I tread along these nightly shores
Foolishly awaiting the sentimental murmurs of a forgotten love
So, the pain that fulfills my heart may understand a once known peace
Even if that peace is to the length of an uneven sigh

Sometimes I have found myself gently speaking of your name
As those soft breezes bashfully flood the lunar-lit sky
Also, I sometimes lose myself to the thoughts of your revered essence
While trailing these memories that are lost to a passionate adolescence

...Oh my dear we had such fire in our souls...

Perhaps one day those wandering planets will align
Together for a short time will our souls intertwine
As we gaze upon that noble cosmic sight

Allowing us to dream
A dream of us free falling in each other's arms throughout the night
Then, for a night
...Of a sacred silent night
I would not have to say that I miss dearly my beloved star

But until that hour comes may God bless whatever heaven it was that sent you

THE NIGHT SKY

STARRY NIGHT

Priceless perceptional pearls
Were the gems once held in the heavens
But it has been so long since I have viewed the night sky
That I do not remember if they are still there

For my past, has caused me to turn a blind eye to such wonders
Thus, at dusk I walk foolishly looking down
To pretend as if that angelic sight that illuminates the stratosphere
Faded with the forgotten love that I had was once known

And though weak hearted I may peer
I also do so, so that I may never stumble again

Yet some cosmic sound keeps whispering to me
Vivified visual descriptions of beauty
Furthermore, lately do I find myself daydreaming of the stars
And of the white sands belonging to the moon

Perhaps all I need is to see the reflection of a starry night
In a rain puddle beneath my feet
To invoke the emotions that was lost in time
With my now wasted tattered memories

Maybe then I can open my sheltered heart to someone
One who bears a beloved smile and a gentle laugh that can echo in my ears
With a welcoming tone, which could comfort my soul

Yes…

That would be a day that I would treasure
Yet until that hour… that moment
I step lightly and recklessly down this path

For my future is unknown but
I always will hold a wishful hope instilled within my mind
Every time I see the ocean blue rain fall in the night sky…

…Life is but a droplet as fragile as it all may seem

RENÉE VERONA

DIVINE TURBULENCE

Visualize the sight of ten thousand lightning bolts
Heaven sent and shaped as the arrows of Eros
Aimed to impale the core crux of my timeless compassion

I know that if I should ever fall again
Towards the emotions of my heart then this will be set
As a divine retribution fated for my poetic soul

As I will offer to her, the woman I may love, an affection to cut so deep
The only thing that may rival my passion
Would be that of a sweet turbulence belonging to a merciless assassin

Seeing as here stands a devotion that would last a lifetime and of a lifetime, thus after

Truthfully, I wait for heaven's punishment
Because she would be the inspiration of God himself
Whom of which provoked the creator to invoke the creation
That we now know as beauty

But…Sometimes I feel as if I am destined to sit with Lucifer and his devils
Since once I find her
I am certain I will make even the angels and all things holy fall to the sins of envy
Instilling jealousy into their soft and sacred veins with my words

My damnation will be that of my own doing
Tainting such pure beings
Having angered God to ironically mock me with those useless arrows and his wrath
…Still I would humbly walk into this self-infected oblivion; if only to know her

Can you tell me…Why would the almighty create such foolish creatures?

THE NIGHT SKY

ESTO PERPETUA

Sculpted by the same hands that fabricated
The celestial stars that hangs in the night sky

I am forever mesmerized by the masterpiece that stands before me
A work of art that always leaves me in wonder and speechless
Harboring the ability to strip away my ability to define such beauty

For, when I look at you time becomes a forgotten god
That bears the same markings of a fallen angel
Yet, you hold divinity in your right hand
And, your touch to the world is that of a blissful angelic embrace

Therefore, tranquility be stills my soul
As if you were the eye of a majestic storm
As well as the sun with no moon to eclipse your imperial seraphic light

Hence, you are ambient in your own illuminating way

I ask, how cruel and merciless was The Father
To not show mercy to the hearts of man when he created you,
For, what I see in you is benevolent
And, as a consequence, I fear for my weak and vulnerable heart

So, this is as a token of my aspiration, thus my undying admiration
…A dedication towards you - a living Fur Elise.

RENÉE VERONA

RIVEN

The fragmented pieces of tainted glass
Are embedded with the lost irises of your enchanting eyes
Still, as if I was a victim victimized by a bewitching lover's spell,
I remain enchanted by such torn elegance

And though this perception seems all to grim for my ill-fated soul
I will watch, without care,
A thousand sunrises reflect off the brim imperfections akin to
The resonating pupils that had been inadequately and unskillfully instilled

For if that noble morning star so happen to gaze across the sky
Yet your captivating presence was no longer there
A thousand sunsets may as well consume a desolate land

With the shattered remains of that which could have been
Together along the lines of that which should have been

Nevertheless…

Perhaps the reason I look, into your flawed and, yet charming echoing glance
Is to remind myself of how broken I honestly am,
Thus, this truth maybe the only fundamental view holding me to this world

Furthermore, it makes me hope; that if I can fix your divide sight
I can believe in my own luckless tattered renewal
A virtue that keeps me as a fool to this enchantment
But, by chance one of the more tragically beautiful things to be known

Because, a sunrise is just a sunrise a sunset is just a sunset
However, your eyes are the vision in mine that brings a tantalizing affection to my heart
Whereas even if they are riven; they are so in the most elegant of ways

THE NIGHT SKY

A FIFTH DIMENSIONAL CURVE

A fifth dimensional curve bends the black keys
Playing a symphony moonlighting the beauty of Vienna
Creating a sound that illuminates a nostalgic fragile essence
Thus, of my tears a musical elegance to convert light

While orchestrating these perceptional day dreams
Viewing the ingeniousness…once held as madness to the common man, my will

And in my own thoughts I sit as a fool, a jester
Justifying my own insane reason to remember what made love so sane
As at the end of any love
The only chords known are that of a requiem

Thine-ing thin strings a lackluster melody
Composed so dark
It was as if Hades himself was whispering your own demise
Viva Voce (with a living voice) so…sinister and cold

Mocking a divinity that was always revered as everlasting
Using me as an instrument amidst this perpetual score
Having my life…a fading composition to do battle against heavenly holy hymns

Yet, there among the impending, looming… deafening drums `
Between the angelic voices hailing from those sopranos
Tender memories become the bases of my reality – A concert of emotion
Leading up to the climax of it all…that which cripples my passion to feel affection again
The simple subtle words of…I miss her…

…I miss her…
…With every tormented fiber of my foolish heart.

RENÉE VERONA

TRANSFIXED

On a canvas that sits idle in my quiet chamber
I will color crimson a complex coat of red
Thus, upon a moment inked vividly with passion
Pastel paint shall cover this portrait outlined with lead

There a stroke of intimacy laced by the lovely lips of lilies
A bed of tulips to love my dandelion the ferocious daisy…

That was drawn as cherry blossoms onto my heart
And of that bud bloomed beautiful an acrylic boundless universe
Stained with the watercolors of liquid star riches
Which, above the sky drew your temporal image

Therefore, mix hot wax and oil to brush away the imperfections
Stencil in the winged messengers that fly with their triumphant trumpets
Then in a step back admire the she to inspire the world

…Benign may it be benevolent…

This imitation that I call art
A forgery to glorify a flawless living masterpiece whereof my aspiration
Etched from my enamel thoughts

My, I fear this painting will never know what it means to be complete

For in the eyes of an artist his work is always lacking
But you my dear lie transfixed in a realm without a blemish or a tear
The joys of my torment crafting something that must go undone

Such is life I guess so magnificent yet, so unfair

THE NIGHT SKY

SEEDS OF JULIET

Let's falsify the unseen dreams
That moves the spirit and grips the soul
One that melts with hopelessness together lost
In a sea that has been broken by the will of man

With all fear beloved in an ocean of lies
Drowning in the hands of the righteous sinner
The angel that beheld sanctuary
As well as the seven seals of heaven

Blasphemy says the heretic
The act of sacrilege cries an unholy ghost
Yet of the holy, the rarity that blooms, lie seeds of Juliet

So, Look beyond the stratosphere
To understand the glory of it all
Bathe in paradise while swimming in the void

That which cradles a thousand suns, and an everlasting silver sighted moon

Allowing, pure intensity to shatter the immensity that wanes
And from that dwindling essence a dove-like elegance
Will grace this well-known creation

Thus, I stand in awe
Towards this makeshift reality that I have seen
A falsified unseen dream that I know soon will be misunderstood

Still…I see these clouds… and these stars…and like all…
I cannot help but wander
Deeply into this cultivated wonder of an unknown gifted God…

…It's sort of like diving into that of universal tides tied by the intertwining ties of fate

RENÉE VERONA

TWELVE NIGHTS & NINE CANDLES

This grim affliction and this shape shifting sacrilege bares lore upon my heart
Periodically, I have been known to be a man ever so lost to the ideals of love
But, curves collapsing to the limits following the five dimensions belonging to Fibonacci
Are said to conspire spell twining, secret writings… ergo an apocryphon harboring ever thus

There within mystery shall beauty be born of us and forever thusly will it surely loom

Steganography to bloom, for she…the lily, that lies within those thorns piercing my perception
A throne for her, my heart's affection, is what I inspire to make reality in view
A Geppetto reshaping matter string together all the dreams, that are said to be made anew

Therefore, decipher this riddle and you
Shall have her name paired with a phrase written by a Montague,

For, twelve nights only nine candles burned two times the measure of seven
So, that the stars could mimic the image belonging only to one, but of nine,
Twelve nights weighted five tons that of three times thus twenty-two tears fell on the fifth still
A quarter scale life knew freedom's myth to move as a pentacle which was removed from a score,
That held the stars to three times the measure of seven encoding my passion within this score.

Thee everlasting Capulet gripping tight the poison to end my life I'm sure
Perhaps, it's all just an enigma, perchance a whisper of how I adore
Maybe the anomaly escorting a god complex to wander even more…possibly but,
Simply alone I can tell you that words and letters are tied to the numerology that lies before

Furthermore, a gift I am cursed with is infecting my heart's core
Birthing an unspoken sacred lore which I dare to reclaim
As in the nights I am tormented by these pains crippling the crux crucifying my soul

This message I have left for you shape shifts in a grim way to keep me sane
That is ever collapsing with curves following my fifth dimensional thoughts
Periodically intertwining with an idea lost to a notion that is everlasting

Like the twelve nights and nine candles burning two times the measure of seven
So, that the stars could mimic the image belonging only to one…Fibonacci's greatest creation

THE NIGHT SKY

ANOTHER GUILTY HAND

The scorn vivid lies that sit within the misunderstood chambers of my mind
Flow eternally with a sight that has been forever masked with my lividity
To obscure these tantalizing memories
That I have for yesterday's false promises and today's passing hours

Depression is setting in, and I do not know when I had lost my will to smile

It's as if I am at the edge of my own optimism, with roses blooming to a blossoming doom
A rainy mood, there for all to see, although also there for me to hide
Mortified a facial surface painted with a tragic face and agony's embrace amplified
This misery is not what I wish to speak of, but therein resides my only inspiration for a time

…Everything just seems so dead…

Intimacy has fallen into vanity, thus the sanity of our humanity is simply profane
As we no longer comprehend the weight that comes with this word known as "Love"
Or how to love as we once did
So, misfortune tied to losing such an entity creates chaos, therefore chaos ensues and I…
And I am surely another guilty hand to these grim portraits sustained sorely as our lives

Thereby, do I listen to the sounds that swing back and forth from this echoing metronome
Staring peerlessly at the titanium instrument hoping to hypnotize myself into a state of joy
To displace an emotion cascading anguish and distress within my own private fortified studies

…Then, again perhaps I am merely lonely
Maybe, I am seeking subconsciously something other than this realm of isolation
For tomorrows, can be fulfilled with untold dreams
As in the next minutes one could turn back into being an optimistic fool
Daring to fathom his, own untamed, un-tattered, reckless heart…

An act I do not recommend, and you may ask why, thusly I shall reply
Tell me, do these memories that I have of her, will they ever fade away from my empty eyes

RENÉE VERONA

CLAIR DE LA LUNE

Memories screaming from the piece of my fragmented heart
Left to distort the beloved field in view of my own piercing paradise
Are sinking swiftly in the forgotten ocean
Yet, there you stand on sand haunting me…therefore holding me, sweet Abigail

To an everlasting moment that refuses to fade.

Although, my precious Juliet,
The gemstone blessed with eyes filled with ecstasy
A trinket of your love quivers violently in time
Forcibly bending space towards your ungodly will

A shame that these tears I have for our misplaced passion should ever fall

But, what are we if not made humble to the thoughts of what could have been
And, to the fragile sights belonging to our own weaknesses, thereby of mine
What has always been and what always will be you, my everlasting love Albina…

Steganography my treasured princess known as Venita

The Venus held as the Hera of a fool's fortune
I had asked for you to stay with me for one more night
In order, to enchant me as you do,
As to wonder me with lust, as I knew you would leave soon

So, for a lifetime my consciousness could slip back into euphoria
To remain lost to an essence of what maybe as captivating as your name…
Thus, evermore as eternal you are…Forever my dear Clair De La Lune

THE NIGHT SKY

COMETS IN THE PRIMORDIAL SKY

I have seen comets swim across a primordial sky that filled a dull hemisphere with magic
Leaving traces of stardust in their wake, which fell in an extraordinary fashion
And, I blinded with passion cared not for such wonders
As in my mind's madness the utmost enchanting ideas wandered with a lingering compassion

…Everlasting…

A fidelity so heavenly, thus unto thee waiting to bloom sat the essence of every flower
Personifying the spirit of an heiress admired and adored by an Aries and his Arian soul
Intrepid, yet forever lost to a twilight belonging to the mythos of her ambient glow
One that held a perpetual purple tint much like a compelling amethyst stone

…A violet jewel said to manifest from an ancient tale predating the modern ethos…

Therefore, from an eternal echo made benign by the cryptic shine tainting her hazel eyes
I see a woman parallel to the goddess Isis, furthermore within my irises I have found this
That I only stand mummified in moments coded cosmic or symbolic relative to her presence
Look benevolence crystallized for a time, so that I may define a creature that mystifies

However, she who edifies those that remain a bit ignorant to a beauty captivating this new age
One crowned with dreadlocks, the sensation stimulating these cerebral thoughts
It would seem my sub-consciousness screams of her image as a beloved forget me not…Still
More I ask of this compelling hemlock flowing within my veins ascertained as the untamed

For, less mundane day by day this fragile universe appears as I gaze upon this revelation
Even suns gravitate towards temptation as empyreal stars tend to caress her brunette skin
Therein, geocentric she has been, fancy a visual view tied to a world of her wonderment

Nevertheless, thee elegance which brim from this lotus stands as a delicate genesis
That emphasizes a weary heart's enlightenment
Hence, to protest could prove to be perhaps perilous, although only a cretin dares to be so dim
Forgive me paradise's gem, but words often lack the ability to depict such a celestial being…yet

It would seem my attention is simply a creation existing only to appreciate you as a stellar dream

RENÉE VERONA

GOOD MORNING

Good morning dear
There is an ocean of dreams that I have dreamt of you
And in the sky, are pearls that I wish to encrust within your eyes
For, you are the unspoken embodiment of heaven's grace

Good morning my dear
There are the seven seas and seven shades of beauty that you claim
My, if only those diamonds in the sky would become of you I would find grace
As, you are a glimpse of paradise with a story untold waiting to be embraced

Good morning sweet dear
Look out of your window and see the riviere revel at your radiant grace
So, that the gemstones trapped within the atmosphere can watch you smile
To mimic your essence, an elegance that is untouched by time

Now, eclipse a moon that chased the sun and sit with me for a while

My sweet dear I must confess
That I cannot remember the last memory of me saying Good morning to you
Even when I stare into these waters that echo a star's image reflecting a shine
That you, yourself have come to create from the pure bliss of your soul's spine

Forgive me, as mornings are not of the norm, nor of grace is this life anymore

Whereas, those sunny morrows left when you did…thus my eyes trailed with tears
Still, perhaps one of these days, lunar lights will ellipse
Until then, a Good night is what I will say to my dear sweet love to whom of which I miss

With my heart scorned I will say Good night…
Good night my dear, until the next daybreak breaks through this abyss

THE NIGHT SKY

CALYPSO'S ECLIPSE

Eclipse the stars for a moment that may become an hour of tender tidings
As I tell you of a dream that speaks to me tales forever tied to the sighing seas
Under the moon, which is now, suddenly lost to the holy signs of an echoing Virgo...
Vertigo so benevolent, so took me as I dared to stare at this delightful divinity

Calypso was her name

A flower blessed with an ebony shade, furthermore my affection weighted
Allowing time to rest in its own eternal thoughts that seem to fade
As light once concaved began to shine from her in such an infinite way
The sheen she displayed brought tears to the heavens and joy on this day

Therefore, watch these open waves confined themselves unto a ballet

Thus, veer your sights towards a Goddess, who controls spatial quantum tides
Thereby, occasionally flooding the sky with a natural stellar bliss
Think for an isolated second, of all the wonders that could follow a cosmic creature's kiss
One who edifies a turbulent storm raging within the heartless

To understand that true wonderment curves a bit parallel to the oceans
Or identical to a gentle smile, which forms from the delicate ellipse of her mocha lips
Hence, convicted I am I must admit
Transfix I sit amidst this concealed essence perpetuating her fragileness

Such ambiance...

Petrified within my perception, an iris personified to be sincerely fortified
Between the banks drowning in my mind; on an island, which often aligns
To a caressing touch beaming off that unyielding radiant sunrise and standing divine
Your irises clarify those traits among your eyes that beholds such a beautiful soul

Listen Calypso...Sweet dearest Calypso
There is a breeze whispering across these barren shores
Singing so compellingly this captivating aspect tailored to a sense so everlasting
And I believe...I honestly believe that this phenomenal spirit...it may only be yours

RENÉE VERONA

AQUARIUS

On the eleventh night, I saw passion in its purest form
For of the eleventh night she alleviated the sand's zealous fire
With the embers of a desert's flame
While manifesting in time her awaited essence

Leaving me paralyzed to the sparks that dwindled
Underneath the inferno which brimmed from the scorching sun
A devout spirit to luster within an afterglow of my own frantic lust
She was the oasis to ale this fever torturing a torched lonesome soul

Thereby a bit of water on the eleventh night
From the eleventh star as I slept within her bosom

Allowing intensity to strike with a blazing deluge of energy
That I thought I had lost to this unforgiving Sahara,
Therefore, in a swift moment I came to adored her
As she was Sanskrit inscribed among this land as Aquarius

An illusion of death held for eleven days
Until she poured a life sustaining nectar upon my brow
Who was this princess baptizing men in this barren dried up sea
Cleansing them of a scalding, blistering fury

I wish, I wish I could tell you myself
Although upon the twelfth morning she left; carrying my love for her as a payment
Thus, all that really, became of her sacred waters
Was a search for a wasteland hot enough to evaporate these sacred tears

My survival alone only a gift to commit sacrilege how could this ever come to be…

Eleven days will I cry out of passion for her
For eleven days, will I bury my sorrows in these shifting sands
Perhaps then, when I am weary will see her again

Delusional, one can walk treading in this heat I know
Yet, as I journey away from this sanctuary in which we laid
And as my sanity is recalled my memories tend to say

I have done this all too many times
Furthermore, I have seen her image before
My salvation, I feel as if you and I have an unspoken lore

THE NIGHT SKY

LOST SOULS

Each time I stood there
Mesmerized at the pieces of my shattered heart
As they all scattered and dance in the wind
Begging for me to chase them and to find them

Yet how could I
When I, myself felt lost
To this agonizing misunderstood moment that taunted me
One that was full of wonder and charm

As enchanting as the moon
But as dark as the night sky
How could I bring myself to wander alone
For that piece of me that belonged to another

I felt so weak
For anger was my only companion
And sorrow drowned my misguided soul in a sea of bitterness

Still, I endured and searched for what was not mine

Although in time it all became sort of vain
Or more so I lack the motivation
Because the memories started to fade
With the well of tears that soon dried up

Therefore, I casted away what was left of my grief
So, that I could smile at the thought of creating something new
To find paradise… to find….

…Where birds may fly, and where the clouds may drift
A wanderer may wander, although one is not always lost.
Isn't it amazing…you know…the way in which we tend to stumble.

Perhaps this is our imperfection,
And it would seem life can be made more beautiful because of it

RENÉE VERONA

DÉJÀ VU

To be honest with you, I am bit frustrated with you
I am a bit taken by you and the way that your image has corrupt my work
In a time where I thought that I was to forget you, I for a time forced myself to think little of you
Yet, it seems that time has reverted,
Back to a former state of its self, and I am now trapped within this paradox...

One intensely lost to an ocean stars,
Where in my gaze, I am completely drawn rightfully to the optic sight of a Scorpio
And ever more to the colors of these stellar winds, which lie so celeste,
That they paint vividly your anatomy...thus, defining your compelling gravity,
Fabricating a bit more the gentle outlook of a divinity pertaining to thee, beloved human-fabrica

My muse, therefore to be held, surely my curse
As my mind wonders, unconsciously towards the images of your charm
However, this infatuation is a bit tiresome,
Delightfully mind-numbing, as well as somewhat distracting
Nevertheless, my intuition oversees my impulses, and I cannot help but to daydream instinctively

For this reason, watch for a moment as I display you as an entity, a' la magnificent

There flawlessly,
Dressed as an empress adorned elegantly in a violet-like iris dress, brimming of a cosmic essence
Passionate, a plutonian goddess baring a heart expressed as only pure and virtually scarlet
And again, I speak of your eyes,
Those hypnotic eyes that blooms of an old soul, bless of Ethiopian gold
A sheer foretold, absolutely personified, perpetually by the glory cascading from an unknown god

Henceforth I ask, while being captivated by your skin made diamond, will it all pass

These concepts giving way to the notions that flood my ideas which are all regarding you
Perhaps as diligent as they are now, maybe to be quite in sureness they will
Possibly equally, this vexation shall cease to linger...
Allowing me to forget what paradise I saw admits the irises embellished upon a seductive vixen
Although still, I wonder is everlasting ever so, in my willful wonderment and wanderlust

Thereof, then the term "perhaps" will no long be a maybe, and I will simply know
As you must know, the quality pertaining to your beauty transcends that of physical attributes
It's simply who you are that intrigues me in a manner found dearly
Hence, benign so may it be benevolent... moreover...
Unequivocal are the perplexing secret affections to what I bare, that I wish to openly share with you

...Stranger still, I feel a slight sense of an eminent, inevitable deja vu...

The diamonds that were embedded in the night sky
Did not last forever as was once promised
Yet neither did those purifying tears
That formed from the black clouds in my heart

But, inside of us all I have come to find
That there is a star that lingers in the core of our decaying souls
That burns brighter than any sun
And one that holds more value than any of the jewels of heaven

It's an illuminating light
That can never dim or fade into the hands of misery
Since its knowledge of tragedy remains ignorant
Although this gem that is buried within us
Is a fountain of wisdom

I have lost myself to this overwhelming sense of joy
And I can only see things optimistically
Because I understand, as of late, that paradise was never in the sky
But, within myself

Therefore, now I can look up at a thousand starless or starlit nights
And be the moon's endless everlasting friend
Till the end of my days and even until the end of an echoing time

THE DEVIATION

THE NIGHT SKY

AMENTIA

My dearest friend, it has been some time since I stood at your door
I left you alone again and for this I apologize so very sincerely
But there are things that I wish to tell you, tales of wonders I have seen
Like angels as well as higher dimensional daydreams, gods and what some would call atomic beauty

My friend, do you know what love is, my it is a wonderful thing
As gravity becomes an un-hilted commodity once you give into those tender possibilities
Where joy becomes, your life making affection much more than dopamine
I mean, have you ever kissed an angel at midnight when the moonlight illuminated your dreams

Such an event can be quite compelling, hence a bit transcending

However, I must inform you about other details pertain to my absence
Like when I saw time as a stagnate transparency, akin to a hollow spatial plane... evidently
Bending all to gracefully to our subatomic wills, moving ever so slightly... quantum-ly
Being pulled timely by virtual particles,
Which are simply popping... yes "popping" in and out of this reality

...Fascinating...

The madness that we share infinitely as infinity is not a number,
But notion of a number that cannot be reached therefore, it equates to zero
For it is nothing but an idea, nonetheless an idea identical to the answer that formulates light which,
Is ninety nine percent of our conscious biology and ninety nine percent of this captivating cosmos

So surely the universe can have a consciousness too...thus I ask would I call that consciousness God
And the planets and stars particles that grab time that condemns us to this space
That illuminates a place where the eyes belong to an angel become that of moonlight

My Amentia
I hope I have not left you alone for too long... come with me and I will show you
As there is more to see...Amentia...listen, in this life it is not just you and me
I promise not leave your side anymore, for you are my dearest friend until the end to whom I adore.

RENÉE VERONA

SCHIZOPHRENIC NORMALITY

I am a bit troubled by these moments of silence
And, one would think that I have found peace in this quiet state
But, to my misfortune it is quite lonesome when my thoughts are not ranting
As I spend a great deal of time alone in my mind

Peer a gaze within my subconsciousness as a non-stop movie makes films
Playing scene after scene - painting beautiful pictures that were once lost in dreams
Speaking poetry and elevated words belonging to a higher dimensional creed
Allowing my personality to split, thus to slip, further into that schizophrenic normality

Where I argue with a reflection, while laughing hysterically at my own torment soul
Together frantically evaluating the quantifiable make up relating to particles
Far too particular in an outright claim inclining itself to be me...The madman
Viewing visions in the eyes of a genius - cursed by his own crippling madness that no one can see

Although, amidst the calm seas I do look for that turbulent storm

When the psyche knows no rest, making my insomnia thee only night terror to lurk
Still, the vigilance is my closes friend...So fitting it seems that it befriends a nocturnal fiend
A glutton starving hopelessly as I set my sights on the hours of a hopeful moon

Therein the paradigm of paradise do I slumber
Thereof this tranquility do I wait for the paradox
Which may make the silent cry cease as chaos shall reign upon my crown
Unstable and equal to the emotions that fulfills my raging heart

...Know that I am blind to this world; A fool wandering this planet in solitude,
Therefore, with a lack of noise does my reality become a bit dark...
Perhaps, this is why some laugh and smile at the sounds echoing from their own looming insanity
...The joys of being able to hear yourselves think...crazy some would say.

THE NIGHT SKY

EDEN'S TEMPTATION

There in transitions to the idioms that infected my mind
Sit the theatrical story of those
That were tricked into gaining knowledge over
The eternal life that was promised to them

Now they, as I, stand in time forever fools to our own intelligence
Bearing the sins of madness; articulating some deity's unanticipated unveiling of ignorance
Work diligently as slaves in servitude to a vile curse that is of man's absurd curiosity

Which slowly but surely makes a habit of stripping away heaven
Thus, we sadly invent words to interpret this forsaken hell
To create a new world that we may describe as paradise

Arrogance!

How can I understand that which I have never understood, for all that is, was so
An atom of "god" full to the brim with nothing
Except its own free will to study and philosophize about the known universe

A cosmos build upon dark matter infused with the same particles
That forces my heart to drum life into this conscious illusion that I dance for,
More so scream over and hopeless fall in love with

The insanity!

Likewise, are my thoughts those marked as sinister in the nocturnal moments
When the twilight of my discord mingles with the midnight of dreams
I lose myself then to the frantic ideas belonging to the hallucinating vagabond
One drowning in the howling voices festering at his wits; leaving him to crave for a divinity's mercy

I want to know what is this delusion…

The quantum hex that is geared towards a subatomic notion once instilled, but
Bent parallel from the abysmal tides regarding empty space
Which was never implied as everlasting, even though it was always seen as such
Though the meta physics held as science among those intellectual fools

Endlessly it seems, we are searching for a garden fruitful with mankind's unwanted vanity,
However, this is something I wish not to believe…in any case its irrelevant
… Because maybe we gave into Eden's only temptation for this very purpose alone
For what is anything if unaware of self… certainly not godlike right?

…Yet, perhaps our ignorance towards knowledge made us as such…

RENÉE VERONA

HOPE FOR THE DAMNED

Ring the bells of hell
For now, is the time of destruction and war my dear friends
Look to the sky and cradle your spirit in the arms
That wain in the grips of the blood moon

As scurvy dogs lash out relentlessly
So, will we and our brothers of the night
Hail these shadows along with these nocturnal hours
Which chokes the day with a lustful easy

Have you seen our souls, yet
Behind the glass eyes that lie in a forsaken creed
For too long we have lingered... damaged, tainted, and thus forevermore corrupted
Without taking any means from the word

Hence with these unholy hands will the first stone be casted

And of the saints and priest that weep,
Scarlet red rivers will be their undoing
Together with cries that scream from the innocent
A befalling glory will walk with us alone... as we are legion....

This is the incantation that I heard at the doorstep of my own oblivion
In light of this with a sad smile, I shed agonizing tears for these demons
Whereas they were my brothers, scorn with the black flames of purgatory

Choose me to torment I prayed, choose me to bare their pain
I will understand,
For, though I cannot wash away theirs sins; I can help them carry these burdens
So, that the souls of the soulless may find a forgotten place called paradise.

I will be a humble vessel,
That will endure the crucified sounds of their sorrows without judging their flaws
For I am as broken as them, but I stand lost in sacred serenity
And because of this my dear father, I relinquish what is left of this life
To restore hope among the damned

To what does it mean to be a saint...To what does it mean to be a human...?

THE NIGHT SKY

BEFORE THE DAWN

It was before the dawn when I stared at this literal shadow of my former self
And sewed into my skin was the un-repented shame masked as my hopeless sin
Lost in paradise then, the frozen wasteland that I now wandered in
Became defiled as my mortal soul was possessed by God's beloved abomination

Weep only at the grave was Death's final whisper

Traverse the inferno as a night fiend corrupted slightly by harlot hands
Screaming vanity towards that everlasting moon
As you embrace the frigid winds beating from Lucifer's black broken wings

For, I have become scum that has been absolved in the blood of heathen gods
A sultan that lingers in the silence which belongs to creations last breath
Sub coming to cruelty while dining in the tomb of heresy
Labeled as heaven's heretic declaring divine mutiny be stilling chaos among the cosmos

Although, Judgment reigns

What was once a pool of gold, became a sea burning with forgotten vitality
Kings and queens lived long behind these walls that fortified the city known as Dis
Thus, I akin fell right in place… a grim mockery to what I claimed in life

…Or rather what I stole from a life

Yet, am I to blame for the verdict
That lies along the treachery of these illegitimate hymns
Tied to self-accusations and vivid unwanted memories
Bound forever to a plutonian deity… yes…I believe so…I believe that I am

Because when time weighted heavy I lacked the required faith to believe in myself
Giving into quickly immortality that was simply presented to me
Something like a forbidden fruit, so sweet but that of a poison clementine…

The air reeks with our agony… our unappealing suffering
More so we are blinded by the sight of our future torment and past transgressions
What I fear most is that I may never know what it means to love again
Sadly, there is no sleep here… just fragile fools wandering around these circles of hell.

RENÉE VERONA

INFERNO

Purge with fire the proliferated personas
That scared the sacred gates of purgatory
And of those that breathe the devil's dogma
A heritage of hatred will devour your soul

For the anger that lies within
Is only one of seven ways
To enter the nine realms that encircles this elaborate hell

Yet, with a hellish fury will you walk
Tainted, and low
Together alongside the demons
That was once created by your lustful immorality

So, under the watchful eyes of Lucifer
Beneath the cold beat of his unholy wings
Salvation will seem but a whisper among this forsaken pit
Furthermore, all that which in favors hope shall be rightfully abandon

Look to God amidst this hellfire
Cry hymns of terror beside your fallen brothers
To instill the truth that echoes between deaf ears that you are damned

Misguided fools we are…Perhaps lost jewels belonging to heaven we maybe….

Because freewill seem so much like a gift
Until we realize how much we are cursed by it
For the one known as Satan does not make us sin
He merely presents sin
It is us ourselves that consumes the forbidden fruit

Thus, we stand as those praying…
Striving for a path of redemption within this tormenting inferno…

THE NIGHT SKY

GALVANIZED BY A DEMONIC STARE

Galvanized by a demonic stare compelling I know for sure
The sinful sounds of revenge they say blood and more blood, so impure
Allow me to introduce myself...excuse me for intruding

I am he who walks in the darkness alone
The devil to his own angelic mind
So, among all, fear with despair are my only allies

Nightmares flooded with screams is paradise unseen
Therefore, sit with me as we burn forever in a man-made inferno
Together, laugh with me at the wonderful sight of destruction curing a human disease

Can you not see you poor, poor fools
An apple is all that it took
And river streaming with rivers of woes covers this afflicted planet that we call home

Praises to our ambitions
Heaven sent are our dreams
Dance with me, DANCE, in this nocturnal phenomenal creed

Let's be heretics
Let's be Satan's legion to be sacrificed parading wild and FREE!
Where is the FIRE in your soul
Show me that FLAME that you hold to be

Imprison yourself, as well as, doubt your deities
Furthermore, lie in the endless universe which is only a perceptional lie
To see yourself as nothing, but NOTHING lost in an empty sea

Thus, then I promise
I can tell you with every fiber of my preordained, hell bound, isolated being
That THIS my beloved brother...that THIS my lovely sister
Is a course for our souls that is not meant to be

But, as I said before I am the devil in his mind; Could you ever believe me
...For a moment let's pretend I have a heart, it brings my suffering a little ease

RENÉE VERONA

THE MEPHISTO

Let's ascertain the ideas proceeding from a charismatic villain
A diminutive eulogy dawning the early signs of a sublime madman...Who was...
To bare the symbolic markings of Alpha and Omega along with a cryptograph telling
The whereabouts of a fallen god's ashes said to absolve a woman's love and a man's lawless sins

Look to those isles belonging to the demi-martyrs
And, there will manifest a manifestation mimicking the one known as Mephisto
Or Mephistopheles, not to be rude, although if one should please
I maybe a devil, but my dignity is still of me...therefore

Shake the helms of serenity for the sake that saves salvation's quoted creed
Dare to dare a venture down the river Styx with me, perhaps a chalice full of wine for thee
As we barrel though the perils which lie unforeseen
Accursed black waters tainted by black souls will be our guided; do not give into your sympathy

Have empathy, yet know that they are there, because of their own anger and selfish greed

Those furious fiends notoriously boiling and burning without brimstone
Maybe, if I had heart I would say that the sight is somewhat of a tragedy...I'm jesting
The cretins trapped in a perpetual state of immorality
As this is the only way that their consciousness can survive, A genocide to thrive

Yes... still I would like to invest in you a sort of hope... a notion that sparks of tranquility
Grip tighter that chalice once given,
And stare at the wine you sipped so slowly to see a liquid ebony...Then,
Hear my incantation which spills ongoing rhetoric thus verbiage concerning your saintly ways
Preaching how you are not bound to this place, nonetheless the river's waters are now within you

To the world I set you free, for hell is not a place for purity
Just remember it is your choice in what you choose to be...Even if a devil has poisoned thee.

THE NIGHT SKY

ONCE UPON A SILVER MOON

Beloved is the sight of tomorrow to the dreamer that dreams away those horrid thoughts
Charmed overly casually, these tainting nightmares pertaining increments of reality
For, here we are in a foreign land, that divides infinity perfectly
Corrupting our fading dominate, addicting personalities, stemming as the bane of one's sanity,

Therefore, within lies a humble lie

Dressed heavenly the profanity, belonging to an articulate cluster of atoms, found crucified
Benign within a nebula of neurons, edging a bent inverted space-time
So, dive a bit deeper, to cause the consciousness to strain
See, all that ever was and will be, maybe all to vain, a poisonous truth in my veins to claim

What I dare to deny, tomorrow's unwanted shame
A dreamer I am, screaming at these hollow tides,
Crying crimson tears as my scarlet eyes defiles the ambient sky,
Thus, became I baptized in my fury for a lifetime

However, an eternity in hell seems more of a fitting compromise
…And so shall it should be, at the end of my time…

Being that, just because a sinner repents, it doesn't change the fact that he was still a sinner
And, just because one dreams of heaven's glory, it doesn't bring such glory that much closer
In truth, its gluttony lost to the mind compelling, some if not all sated fools, who live like swine
Drinking carelessly the devil's wine, forsaking their own anointed ancient bloodline

…Or at least this is what I believe…what I choose to believe

Courting a false final fantasy as we so arrogantly proclaim it to be
Surely, we were meant for more,
Dreaming so, as we dance weeping-ly within this emotional downpour
A lifetime spent to never know if we are truly alive

… Thee irony weighted as the price to balance out knowledge…

For once upon a silver moon, Mephisto gave unto us a forbidden fruit
Take we did…Now naked we are…
Although, this conniving act played upon by a serpent, proved that we have always been
Thus, simply we were shown that we were forever so…

In a tragic way, it's sort of beautiful
…Much like being poisoned, if I may say, by a sacred perplexing truth…

RENÉE VERONA

BEYOND THE BLACK PAINTINGS

Disregard this disposition that is very attentive to those proclaimed disenchanting vows
Let a sultan watch as a poor man hangs, likewise torment he who asked why and,
May I stand mortified, veering at galleries lost to an image persecuting the righteous
Lawless thus, I must inquire bloodshed and to what purpose is it to defile the dead

... It's the proper insurance to behead they said...
Eliminating a perchance, but all I saw was another devil that danced

Say a prayer my brother thy executioner is to come swift
Smear a sneer across these canvases which portrays the subtle ironies of life as a gift
As a sublime subatomic tension submits to a soul substance becoming so surely subterraneous
Curious, I have become to these ravines that peak over this foreign peninsula

For in the moonlight there are shadows that make norm this never-ending sense of insomnia

Therefore, Francisco tell me, what do deaf men hear
Perhaps, only the sounds of perception illuminating in one's artistic eyes
...Although, that's if blindness doesn't apply;

Thorns transformed into a king's crown I believe it could be so
I suppose, expose the if, so-s and a rose shall petal gold... ergo

If a duke then so a prince pictured in this portrait, hence a flower for my duchess
One that blushes at my sweet words, such daunting words that perpetuates my illness
A man whom of which envies the colossuses adrift in his own dreams
Who without reason or sentiment things battled a fierce domestic internal beast

Consequently, what was left was flesh and blood staining these moments she now mourns for
The darken edges grip ever so tighter...The false priest will soon face the inquisition
Night crawlers and flying fiends feast freely on a dying man's woes
So, magnify your throne, beyond these black paintings if to find beauty among the Caprichos

THE NIGHT SKY

ANDROMEDA THE DEVIL'S VIOLIN

Beyond the observed an epidemic plagues the blissful hands of Andromeda
The sad sight screening dying stars screaming
As supernovas pierce that beautiful moon-lit sky

In view a soul lost within the obligations tattered to his own lucid sanity
For filled with vanity is this life thankfully
Seeing as how falsified sentiments make dying, like those stars, an ungraceful thing
I wish I had more time to digress but nothing is as it seems...

War torn is this body and the ever so act of reasoning

Still, there is but one journey this old severed soul needs to make
Because in my years I have played the role as God's grand Inquisitor
Inquiring heaven's purpose and my means to exist
Yet, only gardens grew, as well as did the sun shine thusly so and benign

Although trick question...
How does one question that which knows all?
It's sort of like challenging fate wouldn't you say?
Nevertheless, I ask what would say life be like without an end of days

...glorious I believe some would pray

However, being awake without a means to sleep could be maddening
Frightening, down right daunting, agonizing and more
As all would fade but you...you...which is holy would remain
Lonesome together echoing with pain
So much pain that only your will to love and to create may aid

Therefore, intensify the sun among a fortified hopeful embrace

To burn brightly because, all you may ever know is a dark dismay
Creating to have anything but nothing to forever stay
And despite thy efforts turmoil's lackluster light shall only lay
For, ages and eons as your creation's destiny is to waste away

...Such a joy to have this sweet fruit known as death as my calling
Since falling into eternity is something like walking into a golden prison
And, I will leave that to a foolish God

Understand, that we are perhaps simply whispers
Beloved for a short time by a lonely omnipotent being
So, Sound the devil's violin that plays a keynote to this fiddle's scripted dying creed

RENÉE VERONA

THE CRESCENDO

Among these distorted anti-prisms, the singularity belonging to a multiverse whispers in echoes
And very intricately does a beloved God play the delicate sounds of heaven's symphony
While perplexing an orchestra vibrating vibrantly of mainly quivering quantum stings
Deviating from an apex tied to a mangled matrix, yet like Orion's Bellatrix is it only bound to beauty

Maestro if you will,
Compose a sight unto the world that gleams freely a fifth dimensional gold
To illuminate the grand souls made of sol
That interprets an enigma causing bent space to be labeled as a nomadic perpetual time
And, in thy own eyes shape a shifting photonic light that has been encrusted with diamonds

While sharing parallel particle like pearls
As those electrons and gravitons intertwine in an unlikely fondness
Honest, have you ever danced within realms of elevated dimensions
Traversing the galactic ley lines
In such a fashion to have your entire being thus remedied with passion

Lost to cosmic madness, staring deeply into a stellar abyss as your celestial veins franticly pulsate
Intune to the chaotic order of all things created benign between the minutes of creation
Forever to think that something all to perfectly profane could become so purely profound

That even a three-head hell hound could find grace
And momentarily look up peacefully at that broken sky

… A notion to reach ever densely unto that light bringer too…Ergo

Expect a melody measured by those harmonious sighs of supernovas
That glares universally into the arctic voids proceeding from those black holes where I lie
Mimicking a crescendo personified but paralyzed to the music that intensifies
As those lullabies upholds the essence of Virgo

The principio once more stands convicted towards those convoluted impossibilities
As a covenanted I paint so vividly across the empty spatial canvases eloping within my mind
Blind to the complex wonders simply eluding mortals that remained as the unwise
To what purpose is it all,
If I die not singing with these holy hymns and chords amplified by the crucified

Specifically deriving from Andromeda's violin, and for it listen, a din vision
A bit of paradise I gaze upon
…Which fades slowly although surely objectifying this fragmented life of mine…

THE NIGHT SKY

SOUNDS OF THE SAMURAI

"My brother in hell we shall share a drink
My brother in hell we shall know peace
And who so ever among us shall die first, may his bother follow him swiftly"

These were the words I agreed upon as we stood as enemies
As our swords dared to dance in these broken forsaken winds falling hastily unto the east
For, in a time of war our bloodlust grew knowing only gluttony
Therefore, agony fell upon those that viewed themselves as brother tied the impending hostility

Gradually, let me reenact a scene cemented in trails and tragedy

Look to the sky as the heaven's tears episodically stands to fall upon two spirits
Lost to their half-hearted ambitions that drown in each other's blood
Hold the sight of lighting screaming from their brittle blades
Every time they dared to draw the others last breath, piercing violently with a striking tempest

"Dine with me brother in the glory of our rivalry"

What valor they knew when a burst of adrenaline corrupted the veins
Man-slayers dreaming only of the next moment, entranced only to the conflict
Sinister steel grazing flesh and bone simply adding more excitement to the calling of their own deaths
Such a small price to pay they believed as they echo actions in this misguided paradise

Although, perceptional-ly a paradise nonetheless
One to awaken thunder from its somber silence, feeding off the energy raging with intensity
That became that of dragons storming throughout the same heaven's crying so endlessly
Dramatic timing sharp edges cutting carelessly, as both daydream fittingly about the other lobotomy

"Come, with me brother, do not dishonor me"

In this horror as some would call it, these samurai found a profound peace
In this fantasy, they discovered an innocence, which only they seemed to understand genuinely
It was if they were playing, and death was an un-feared penalty
The chaos grew, dragging on for what seemed like an eternity
Allowing for hours to pass as cherry blossoms hoped to bud anew, but only a fatal iris bloomed

"My brother in hell we shall share a drink
My brother in hell we shall know peace
And who so ever among us shall die first… my brother…My bother I am sure to follow you swiftly"

RENÉE VERONA

OF THE RAIN

This rain…This rain entails of a story
Belonging to a lonesome man lost to his own shadow
Whereas, he had been blinded by himself
With the entrusted sheen of his own light

So, when the thunder would sound
His heart would skip a beat
Allowing lighting to surge throughout his body somewhat freely

Therefore, unto these dark clouds would he remain as a jolt of wonder
As well as a stone to these heavy winds
And, like a God would he stand tall towards this ill-fated storm

Walking amidst this downpour as if
The holy waters that fell from the heavens were a part of his soul

And of a demon he would seem to some
Because, within this raging undying torrent
He would sit as its indestructible heart

The crucified crux known as the devil's monsoon…

Yet, underneath the broken tears that fall from the sky
Together beneath the elegant silver enchanted moon
This rain…This rain would flood the man with an everlasting ambition

In light of his own shadow
That any storm would be nothing,
But, a manifestation of the tears he had held within, so…
As long as he internally cried, so long would any storm seem as such

…Hope is what the rain brings to the man
For you see, in time even the rain would eventually know its own end

THE NIGHT SKY

A GALE LIKE PRISM

The elemental outburst claims forces brought out by the winds of a hurricane
For they may carry out the sorrows of the past that sits within a lock hearted monsoon

Make shifted unto the unknown whispers of tomorrow
Those that fill the air with a gale like prism akin to a gem that radiates with the color of green

Yet who could know all the hues that flood the sky
Under the heavens and among the heavens
And of the earth that bears scars towards that of a sacred tempest

Unimportant I presume
Whereas I the forgotten vortex of time
Looks forward as to dance with gusto in these cyclones of hell
That echoes with the drums of life left breathless by a careless tempo
Therefore, I stare recklessly at the typhoons that move with the same sinister notion as me

Although, a breeze could clam my wild and untamed nature
The violent storm that rages within would not understand those gentle ways
Thus, condemning my essence to a whirlwind of emotions
Marked with the same chaos that instill a lost zephyr

You see, All I have herein this life lies forsaken within these winds
That sit above the clouds frozen in the stratosphere as a poetic ominous god

So, take my hand and I will show you how to fly
Grab the diamonds that where mistaken as stars
And we will drift attuned to an intertwining flow
One that sways with elegance between these everlasting unwavering winds

RENÉE VERONA

A HYMN OF LIGHT

A hymn of light to welcome me home where citadels glimmer gallantly of blue sigils, so vivified
That logically I must incline that this moment seems very much like a fantasied dream
For last I remember the chronicles I embarked upon had lingering signs pertaining to vitally

Therein, I should digress about my synthetic sins,
However, this view conspires with beauty, my friend

Envision a world forbidden and, therefore locked away
From the broken irises plaguing the narrow minds found within those corrupted mortal men
Moreover, let me describe unto you the magic brimming off heaven's enchantments,

Thus, fabricate a miracle to realize the truth regarding this fascination...That

A gate encrusted with pearls is merely the beginning, simply an introduction preluding the immensity
Picture dimensional colors raining from an angelic ether, scaling the spiring atmosphere
With every shade mystic and arcane, free as if they were absolved out of the feeble prisms
That we ourselves often mistakenly imprison our fragile selves into

...Self-sealing gems we are, our transgressions lie as proof...

Nonetheless or nevertheless, I must continue foretelling solely, if only to enlighten you
That spellbinding art these astral temples covered in sapphire crystals echoing a diamonds charm
Concealing the revealing relic stones
Burning with an afterglow which, gives stars their fluorescent shine
Subsequently, Seers exist as flying spirits singing songs sanctifying solar seraphic sanctuaries, thereby

I must admit man's riches compared to this appears to be terribly dull, together surely irrelevant
As I ask who cares for gold when paradise sit at the ends of one's fingertips
Visualize energy colliding with mending personas causing the pinnacle of a soul to levitate
Preordain to the ritual concerning life's fatal exchange could this be our next profound consciousness

So, waits for me these ambient hues of heaven dancing majestically like beloved quantum fairies
Breathe with me, my last breath as I fade into ecstasy... A hymn of light to welcome me home
...I die my friend, but please forgive me as I leave you in this war filled world all alone...

THE NIGHT SKY

LILIUM'S REQUIEM

Let the perfect lily bleed
For as it dies so will the sorrows that I harbor
Those that illuminate within the wasteland of my heart
In which blooms within the fading glory of a daunting fragile light

No more is the sight of terror
In the eyes of he who is masochistic

But praises to his lords, and to the judges of his relinquished retired soul
For they are the gate keepers of his eternity
One that is sought to be a labor of hell and a longing reach for paradise.

I have seen the sacred scars of my everlasting damnation
Yet, I do not fear a fraudulent view of discord
Not even one promised by an unknown god

For I am a master of my own cursed providence
And rather a demon or an angelic servant of a higher being
I thus walk shrewdly down my own forsaken path

Therefore, I care not of the hate that may come towards me
Nor of the love that may instill me
Only that I continue and that I endure

So, that I will strive beyond death in spirit or other ways to transcend past this fleeting life
A life that is a draining flawless illusion of time
An appendix that will last only until the next moon

My dear dying lily you are nothing but, A silent note that belongs to a requiem
That breeds in the minds of those that are franticly conscious

… Lilium, the Metaphor to my Life…

RENÉE VERONA

A NIGHT OWL'S KISS

Let's peer into the hideous, marauding, discord of my feeble, and wretched mind
As a prelude towards a sinister gesture
An invitation that beckons the enchanting dance of a dark waltz

For beauty plagues a charming volvere
Although it also, seems to taint the realms of my nocturnal dreams
Which in lies scarlet petals that were scarified to the forgotten
And evermore to the emerald irises of the woman that I could have loved

Much like the broken beacon bound by my devotion that is forsaken, but beside it
A night owl stares infectiously within the grips of my slumber
A creature who had no fear towards a ghostly raven
Whom of which cried of an echoing terror, haunting with the words of "never more"

Subsequently so is this vanguard-ing vagabond.... yet,
Fibonacci, oh Fibonacci rings amidst my ears
Manifesting itself in all as the gold means to our fading existence
Thus, are these ratios of doubt, for I too have lost my muse and my purpose to live

Therefore, upon the wake of this earth
And through the sudden pauses that mar the delicate universe
I await peacefully for the reaper to share a dance with me

Hereinafter, in view my downfall with this thorn
To what is life without the gaze of wonder, furthermore what is inspiration
Hence let the red rose bloom without petals born befitting sacrilege
Nevertheless, as time become that of grim's together in time will stand

As I flirt with lady death upon this eradicating ballroom floor
Her kiss will seal my fate
One that I welcome because she is my true love...

The forbidden apple that hangs at the door of my oblivion
I will step with her in circles for the ritual that lifts the spirit from the body
And with bliss will I lose what it means to be a mortal man
Thusly by the virtues of a night owl's kiss do I relinquish my soul

THE NIGHT SKY

A LATIN EXPRESSION

It's a compelling cold embrace guided by hallowed hollow graves
An inescapable profound responsibility fragmented as an inadequate relic;
That is meant to be forgotten
So, steady is the sedative sedating these ongoing lucid moments, which we speak softly of,
Yet, hang from the gallows for, and with our dead language pray only about

In turn we suffer within our own self infecting agony
Thus, we share the same tormenting outlook of demons for a time
While, reaching ever so dearly for grim's angelic hand throughout these dim nocturnal days
Shape shifting in a sense, hoping that some form may allow us to become god's holy martyrs

But, it would seem,
That alone shall stand a self-entitled arrogance and thy own beloved ignorance

A pity I would say as some echo in the lost shambles waking among those paranormal eclipses
Although, this all lies in favor to those manners
That are portrayed by that which is supernatural
Still, I must convey that what is not unnatural is this ideal known simply as memento mori

For, even if one could grab lighting from the heavens to resurrect a corpse;
Time lingers perpetually upon death's non-derivative side...

Are we really, not but clay sculpted by generations of evolution I wonder
If so mankind's greatest fear should be the chilling whispers belong to extinction
Perhaps this is, why we cling to the concepts pertaining to those everlasting beings
...or a forever living...all
As they...these thoughts give off some sort of hope, that one day we could be as such

Truthfully, I find that notion to be a bit self-centered and cowardly
Nevertheless, I am of that hopeful lot,
Because, even if my body may perish I don't wish for my consciousness to be so fleeting

Memento mori
A Latin expression... for all life... merely meaning... "Remember that you have to die."

RENÉE VERONA

THE DOGMA OF AZRAEL

Sweeter than the taste of honey may our final conclusive hours be
However, this impending requiem tends to invoke louder as my heart beats more
And upon my ears I can hear pulsating blood vibrating whispers of fears within my mind,
Furthermore Listen,
Dissolution comes dancing for the culling, smiling while gripping tightly tremors tied to tragedy

Such a bane score, so quietly personifying a fatal phantasm that we subserviently wait for
Thus, mentally run from, as to dream optimistically about the uncertainties regarding eternity
A memento mori lingers, although perhaps it will all fade into a blighted eye stained with obscurities

Wishful thinking…still, I propose Socratic thinking… that of "what ifs" and "whys"

As if, what if this creature that hunts our very lives, only does so to understand why it is alive
Condemn forever as a lonely presence, living vicariously through the tales we tell as we die
Guiding us away from life's lies when we become decrepit and mortified,
Vivified is death's sacrifice…To give generously something which a reaper can never receive,
…Our ever-blooming misconceived mortality

Tell me, would you ever think divine beings yearn to escape an existence bound to a bleak infinity?
Could we be angels consciously subsiding herein a mortal dimension
To forget for a moment our divinity hoping desperately that this everlasting prison,
Which we are chained to surely does not last perpetually
And that liberation comes hastily, as we crave the knowledge of a beloved, and poetic peaceful end

…I ask is that not also providence…

How many times has the creator created the stars that we see while the night sky oversees
Give unto me a number…
That equals to the countless parallel universes composed at the foot of God's throne
For what is time to an immortal, but a concept held scared unto man
Nevertheless, revel for a second at this flower…adore this notion which sits more precious than gold

Inconceivable to think that we were deliberately constructed this way as to waste away
To meet that grim persona whom about I spoke of before, yet
Possibly, we expire and the stars collide so God can perceive those gears belonging to time as we do
Therefore, cherished novelties here a physical fantasy we might simply be… Hence, the ideology

The dogma of Azrael,
Who waits endlessly as heaven's faithful time keeper, one always feared and always lonely

THE NIGHT SKY

METAMORPHOSIS

It all starts when you accept the reality of your death in your dreams
You fade with the smoke that you exhale
And you stand in the den of your own soul

You are blinded consciously
Because subconsciously your third eye peers at all that is unknown
While drifting in this limbo it becomes all to surreal

Then is when you realize
That you are no longer in your physical body
Therefore, franticly you start to understand a measure

The weight of how lost you are in this fragile existence

Fear subdues the weak minded
With the illusions of astral demons hunting the heartless

For only with an unwavering heart may you tread in these lands
These nocturnal psychedelic fields
Or you will be forced to deal with the devils that lie within

The likes of which that can leave men chanting
And saints praying for a god that may never come
Thus, forsaking a society built upon blasphemy

Though things become clear once nothing becomes your ambitions
But you walk with the will of the universe as a new-found glory
Allowing that past fear to shift into a feeble irrelevance

Now, watch as this fruit opens all your chakras as you have a spiritual metamorphosis
 You will see the heaven that surrounds us all
With a new aura that will protect you from an ongoing hallucination.

RENÉE VERONA

PROPHECY

Embody the seven seals
Sealing the echoing quatrains revealing the prophecy tied to revelation
Stare deep into the eyes of a white stead that screams vengeance
Throughout a great city known as Babylon

There a beast looked upon by seven stars and seven angels
Will bring war, famine, conquest signifying death cloak as the dreaded four horsemen
Thus, when the earth shakes his time nears
When the sun burns of black flames will the heavens cry celestial tears

Then will God grip lightning bolts, and from his wrath
A universal whisper akin to an electrical magnetic pulse is to come
A destructive wave destroying man's cosmic satellite systems
Creating comets that claim attributes mimicking mesmerizing metallic meteorites

Therefore, in the days which knows the night chaos is to bloom – seven trumpets to sound
Announcing the sacrificial lamb to say that this is but, of the first seal

Those that are to be the fallen, upon their right hand as well as their foreheads
A man's face which lies with gold will be imprinted
Whereas, in their works they only sought out the treasures of man
Thereby of their mind their mind's eye became blinded by the gilt

The root of all evil potent symbolism making sense within a poet's optic sight

A welcoming throne stained with genocide befitting an empathetic villain
Thee antichrist looms among thy soul…poor sinner held to the legion
One belonging to many, although many of one
Still, nature tends to sing in a form much like a duet…so; to change is but a simple act

For, I believe even Lucifer can appreciate the beauty of a butterfly
But, the devil tends to takes that beauty, and proceeds to strips away its life
These entities that we call everlasting rest only in our choices
Choosing as humans to personify them as to shed away some of our guilt

In regards to what one may have done or
Having the intelligence to know that one exist, however being unable to know truly why

Armageddon is an internal battle,
That if lost by too many of mankind could cause extinction to our species…
…Prophecy, the telling of destiny can be easier to see when someone's hands are unclean

THE NIGHT SKY

CANTO 79: THE ALCHEMIST

Alchemic expressions will linger within these verses of mine
That transmute symbols into knowledge
Seeking desperately for the evidence tied to an equivalent exchange
Which is not a law, but a promise… A subatomic bond created from emotions like that of love

Something once so sacred to the human psyche,
Yet now, the main sacrifice to sacrilege among man
Horrible it all seems, as the blood which justifies dying personas seeping ever so grimly
Through the equinox of an elegant hourglass timing dearly the creation of a philosopher's stone

The magic vindicating Von Hohenheim's blessings and Newtonian gravity

Therefore, Hermes grip tightly a guarded chemistry once foretold
As distorted eyes stare deeply at the edges of religion's threshold
Solely to comprehend the science belonging to the Greek gods of old

The mythos pulling about the element sol,
As the Luna loses its soul; A Venus shall wait for a king
Predating the pyramids along with all other things…Shamefully, society's new universal three
Those that were scripted unto these emerald pages buried deeply beneath Egyptian gold
Dogmatic principles and verses whispering a heretic's fatal final woes

…Equally ancient ties above and below…

Living abominations unable to escape their own logical minds
Known as thee envious homunculi prideful-ly claiming a lustful truth reforming self-greed
Subjecting one's spirit unto retribution thereby of Elohim's wrath, if one should ever believe

That divinity is an attribute imbued within all, thus all is divine…Although why,
I must ask is philosophy such a heavenly crime; or perhaps it's an experimental trial
A quantum step…
A sanctified scientific method geared towards opening the doors to our immortality
But, is eternity worth anything if a being suffers such forever alone

…The vanity of infinity I suppose

Nevertheless, look ahead for into gilt will I convert Saturn from lead
Purposefully, as I am thee, and thy rings reign throughout heaven as my own cosmic halos,
So, sing with me these lines tied to the words canto seventy-nine
As angelic mortals become a variety of lights by virtue of a periodic prism
Refining life transparently benign to have algorithms burn against those biblical brimstones…

The true gift of the alchemist maybe their enlightenment
A symbolic formula made metal and esoteric like your unequivocal soul

RENÉE VERONA

ROYAL EYES

Turquoise… It's a calming color rooted in my mind
One that is lost in the greenish blue hue falsifying these nightmares of mine
But, I do not care for the fallacies of my reality as the lies keep me grounded within
So, I do not chase a broken spirit sins that dissipates in the wind

Life can be very transparent at times, yet astoundingly, profoundly unclear

…Ironic I guess…Still, I wonder if…
You can tell me why these flowers reach for the sun before they wither and die?

As it all just seems so mediocre, dull, and vain
No matter how colorful their petals may blossom
It only comes off as another shade of grey
Looming with a somewhat artless eeriness that surely doesn't fade

…The pessimistic cloud storming with a downpour that no one cares for
Drifting beneath sunbeams and shine

Truly pathetic, not knowing that it could throw lighting from the sky
The trumpets would sound and its thunderous voice would cry …what a shame
As a bit of courage does wonders when we tend to fly
Furthermore, the raging hues of a garden inspire the galactic stars to intensify

Crack open the heavens and rain down the reign of the four horsemen with a sonic boom
Lift the veil that covers a biblical revelation as you crawl towards your own doom
For the Apocalypse, Armageddon, as well as Ragnarok
Are just petals adding symmetry to the same flower that blooms

Optimism is relevant, although you wait for the inevitable and I ask why?
Life has a tranquil beauty to it; you just have to open your royal eyes

THE NIGHT SKY

A NAME UNSPOKEN

What has become of me...Do I dare stare at the un-wanting sky
That which lingers in a field of solitude that shines of false promises

Who am I to question the consciousness the breeds from nothing
One that is unparalleled to self, and only mirrored by the naive thoughts of a child

Truly it's an unspoken hill with no name

That floats in the atmosphere
Where the earth and the moon may touch in the arms of the cosmos
While fading under the light that belongs to the sun

I ask

Can one pull me from my silent curse
Moreover, save me from the abyss that is of my own image
The sight of a beast with a heart that is chained to the unbroken walls that are bound to hell
Those that art held up by the sins of a loose, and frantic aging mind

Alone blessed with the grace of heaven to forever see fire
And bleed tears that are dyed with the color crimson

For nothing but the weight of my own emptiness, together with the darkness of the world
That is confound by the name of a beloved God that has yet to be aesthetically known.

Everlasting it would seem
This yearning that would never seem to be fulfilled
Therefore, with this notion I believe that it's a mistake
That I might ever strive to want as I stand unwavering in this sense of a holy perpetual awe

RENÉE VERONA

A SILENT SYMPHONY

Have you seen it…the falsehood of your salvation
And the requiem that strings along the sound of your dear, dear sanity
An instrument that was played by the hands of demons
And well composed by the devil himself

Take to the stars that fall only in the night
A truth belonging to the illusion once cultivated in a lie
Scared by an unholy holy marked in full to fool the eyes of man

What a cataclysm
A perpetual holocaust that burns the soul of the sinner
Like a lake of fire biblical instilled upon the spirited of man
So, that their minds may never be free to understand the knowledge
That which was planted within the seeds of a well-known forbidden fruit

A punishment some have called it
But perhaps this is why mankind fails to see the sacrilege of their own discord
And a symphony screaming with sorrows is all a sympathetic god must hear
For what else would ring from the hearts of such man

Tragically we are flawed
Creatures that are designed to fold unwisely at our own cosmic purpose
To rage against that Oh so familiar dying light
As fate, that inevitable returning deity drags us into the everlasting impending void

The questions that I pose are these
Are we aware of the nothing that may become of us
Or of that emptiness that makes up all things on a quantum level

A thought I believe only dying angels should ever wonder… or dying gods

Yet, could it be that our consciousness that we carry with vanity
Be the only substance that holds any actual weight
So, that we may bend that nothingness that even our gods could come to fear

And do we dare to drift into that sacred silent unknown…

THE NIGHT SKY

THE AESTHETICS OF...

What do you say to a man that can see though nothing
A person that can comprehend all the poetic formals of space-time
Yet, he himself has no way of proving such vanity

As for years, he had searched not just for god, but of his own self
And in this forbidden journey he has found love, hate, sadness, and joy
And along this sea of emotion no idol stood... only a perception that was ever changing
Vital to the sanity that understood it all, though with it all did it to slip into madness

To think what if
What we have been search for was nothing among nothingness
Every day we peered at the heavens
Looking to see that which is, although is not ever there

Which leads me to this question...How can something be so vast with empty space
Yet, at the same time conscious of every atom that makes up its own personal universe
Structured with intelligence... able thus capable to dream about everything
However, it has no substance merely, lies and illusion cradled in stardust called man

Tell me what do you say to a man that can see the conscious mind of nothing
Who can see the poetic abstract mental state of a void
The fool foolish enough to tattoo the laws of chaotic order upon his skin...

For eons, we will chase after that which can be simply over-stood
Undermining the beauty of it all... The pure genius of it all
To have something needed that can never be found
Something to come before any god and after, since nothing edges that which is everlasting

I guess you can call it the curse of our first sin one that only an all power God could create

In this reality, all things can be formulated, calculated, and represented by numbers
Now of those numbers there is one that has absolutely no value
But, without it everything falls apart...and you can't take it out.
Seeing as how it's the answer to the formula of light itself

Therefore, through it alone everything becomes possible...
A theory – nevertheless I wonder
If this emptiness had a consciousness like you and I, would you call it God...
Perhaps it's a concept most would find troubling, still does it not intrigue

What do say to a soul that believes all things are possible? Even the aesthetics of...

RENÉE VERONA

IMPERFECTION

Shattered shards and shackles
Scattered and bounded to a soul so unfortunate
Lost to an offbeat melody
That can still sound beautiful to a broken man's mind

It's sort of like
Fallen cherry blossoms that seem more enchanting as they fall
Then when they bloom
A tragic whisper that is alluring to those that can understand
The tears of the dying sakura trees for they too have cried

But in an odd way this heart-rending act in life
Plays with such finesse that it captives
And tantalizing memories are formed somewhat everlasting
Equivalent is that of losing love

For its pivotal moment in every creature's existence

Perhaps without these un-savory moments
Or without these undesired scars
We wouldn't know beauty
Because I believe that true beauty lies in the imperfection of all things

Maybe that's why
We think it's perfect in that abnormal hour when we think back
Or maybe this way of thinking is as outlandish as the emotion that I am seeking to inscribe…

…Foolishly described I guess
Yet these falling cherry blossoms that seem so tantalizing are scattered throughout
The memories that I have, and each petal to me is perfect

Each tragedy is just another beautiful scar

THE NIGHT SKY

THE CITY OF THE SETTING SUNS

Gaze into my piercing eyes for a time, where the setting suns tends to die
And I let the hours which are possessed by these meaningless minutes
Pass from the seconds that we hold so dear within a wakeful moment,

One conscious to the cerebral sounds of these visceral elements
Echoing signs conforming to a sense of forever…for an everlasting ever, cannot be denied

See the melody belonging to a city unchained willfully from a mortal parallax
Frozen to an angelic like mosaic painted, descriptively and intricately shouting beauty
Finding cryptography within a broken chronograph tattooed timely of steganography
Holding riddles pertaining to the unseen
Thus, blessed his he, who knows the serenity coursing about his own simplicity

Because that apart, an enigma is the heart
Still, I gazed deeply into her eyes to find what some would call a soul
For lately the nights have been quiet cold, as these beloved stars refuse to shine
However, I discovered something almost divine among the nocturnal tide,

…That there may be another weary just like I…

Resting in the city of the setting suns, watching as the dawn slowly dies
Believing that the morning was simply a momentary lie,
Since, the night was only hiding behind this vile of incandescent light
Such is the secrets shadowed in time,
An epic instant vivified, when we let things fade beneath the twilight

Nevertheless, forsaken I stood unsure to the glory that illuminated life in the heavens
Feeding on an eerie atmosphere, dreaming with ever ticking gear gauging an aging clock
That perhaps space may know an ellipse… as to curve like her nimble lips
Much to a whispering kiss, sighing repeatedly ripples of images tied to unforgotten paradigm

Perchance, but was this the fate of all things I wondered, why must I even try…
Gaze into my piercing eyes for a time,
For in that somber darkness I saw a creation so benign, edging so surely sublime
What I asked was to carry me beyond this cherished night sky…
Where thymes tended to wither, and tended to unfortunately die

A distance voice cried out saying… together we will make it, you and I…
…Together… someday… we shall watch the beckoning sunrise…

RENÉE VERONA

CHAOS ENSUES

What would you have of me?

The savagery that is confounded to the eradicating thoughts
That clings to the open scars in my mind
Or of the benevolence that protects the fading impulses
That echoes, vibrational life from that of my fragile and, yet dying heart

It's a pitiful conundrum that baffles reason
Together does it make a fool of intuition
And, still I stand hopelessly in the midst of the two
Whereas one is eternally careless, and the other forever reckless

But, tell me,
Does the tectonic tyranny of a torment soul
Shed tears for the purified body once tainted by its own ignorance…

…Maybe…

Thus, is it feasible
That a question such as this may stem to the core of all that is chaotic
To all that lingers in a beautiful sense, bound by a divine disorder
Masked as a sequence held only to that of an elegant inelegance…

If so I wonder…

What random events that are star-crossed are so phenomenal
That the beloved angels would fall from the good graces of heaven
Leaving man to search on earth for the cryptic signs God
And is faith all there is left to believe in

Because it would seem

As if faith is the last known parable that was cherished and hoped for
Like an idealist concept lost to some sort of idol or entity…

Perhaps this could be the unfortunate case that lies at hand
Therefore, who I am probably does not matter
Although, what I am could still beg the question

Hence, chaos ensues far beyond this cosmic order
With the sole purpose to cripple a misunderstood universe

A PROLOGUE

AURORA BOREALIS

THE NIGHT SKY

- Aurora Borealis -

There sovereign in our ways we stood noble and true
Contesting those demonic forces with the dawn
And one by one the fiends proved to be fools
Still, facing my surprise I was struck down by a spear;

Thus, I fell from grace...A blemish upon God's face the holy angelic tear

How majestic approaching this earth I might have seemed
As a comet of great awe, a casualty during Tyreal's Great War
When the archangels found so swiftly that they could still bleed
I drowned into man's unsanctified blue sky losing my creed

Dematerialized from the hallowed guardian I once was
My now physical body became that of a king's sword
One trapped in stone for ages   yet, beloved by all

And cared for by a lady bound to an eerie lake's shores

Although, the core of my spirit became tainted
As I was used to massacre those that I was sworn to protect
Whereas in heaven from which I departed   all life under and above is sacred,
Therefore, those akin to the light do not kill we simply subdue

But, take me now the holy weapon of mortal kingdoms
That bestow unto all a reason to hope with vanity
For, as I butcher souls to aid the cause of another
My sacrilege shall soon open the stern gates of Valhalla

Thus, Ragnarok will become a storm upon these poor vital creatures
Much more than I ever was... Much more than I for sure
I the shape shifting key to the doors of man's Armageddon
And of these individuals that I shall curse...shall all sorely proclaimed
That which they echoed with joy in their tales...Excalibur – My triumphant name

The divine item which devils and elevated stars' converse to take
To claim for my essence in this state could tip the conflict
That wages within a fourth dimensional plane...My eternity may stumble in vain

But, old jolts sparks lighting emanating from forgotten gods
The Valkyrie sound trumpets as Odin and sons lie to favor our odds

There in a past time before my fall this is the image of what I saw

RENÉE VERONA

A lone lancer sits in a field blooming with broken blades
Glaring at the sky contemplating his own shame

Adamant and unyielding are the battle cries of his dead brothers
That found his mind a living sanctuary to plunder

We are the demi devils of war, cold steel excites our lust for blood
And the way of the warrior is our path that will complete this calling
They screamed at the threshold of their own culling

…What a portrait ever so vital…
To the history given generously as a mistaken providence

All a memory for the man that held a spear   spared from the impending calamity
Due to the velocity that illuminated his skills as a master of violence
Yet, this well polished art   chipped slowly away at his heart
And the lance that he carried was now a sigil carrying his sins

Tremble at the sight of Gungnir   the bone that invokes a rageful lost spirit

Among the arrows that hailed from the sky
Those that stood as flowers to honor the dead, and their petals that flowed in a pool of blood
There will wandered the embodiment of justice left as a manifestation of pure carnage
How cruel is fate to the man justifying it all…What becomes of his sanity?

A beast he is now, so tragically no one cares to know
Yet, I wonder if pride stands firm when all you dream about is death
Perhaps unknown to those that fear him; This demon might still have a beautiful soul
Thus, honestly he sits alone searching the heavens to simply find a means to atone…

Naive I was to think so in the midst of a war
The impaler stood tall to impale those nigh to his own skin
The backbone of his atonement in my eyes a sigil broken within

Listen to close the dreams of his illusion

Unlimited retribution for the fallen swords that I walk upon
And for every fading face that disappears in silver shine of the moon
Thus, an evolution belonging to my vengeance that edifies a stubborn foe
Moves swift and vigilant to calm the raging beast that I bare

I know not the way of peace
For I have forsaken that path to stand in a field
That bloomed a garden of blades, therefore, to the world I am the persistent will of havoc
A spear known only to the right hand of your death

THE NIGHT SKY

So, Look to the sky

There a dark cloud formed of arrows is the storm I bring
It's the culling that has been invoked by all of those that scream
Witness the carnage of a lone soul
The sword to bend time causing men and angels to fall short of their own

Accelerate the complex molecules that are calling
As cold steel carves a passageway to a threshold of providence,
Stare at heaven and behold   that this is the way that awaits a righteous demon
Seeing how as only gods prevail in war, rather they be holy or otherwise lo...

A smile lingered upon his face, together red optic irises defiled the air
Leading me to lose my anointed place

...Gungnir... Gungnir...

Soon heaven will come unto the earth allowing my body to regain its angelic form
Then you and I will walk in the rain
Thunder shall be the drum of devastation, a loud whisper summoning your unholy name

Bestowed with the virtue of patience I surely await that day
Lavish in that hellish paradise unscathed   for your hour of reckoning that nears knows no delay
The elaborate plot forged by the sisters belonging to fate
Foresaw Tyrael's totality as a beacon in the last days

...T'was time

To tread towards the trinkets   that trembled twining two temporal temples
Twisted three times thee tangled twin tides teeming
Tedious tendencies testifying tomorrow's tied turbulence

Tectonic trigonometry tricked the tantalizing trinity
Thereby tribal tranny tore tranquility
Tempting temptations tatted tiles together to torment thus treachery

Tactless teaching   tell tales truly their theories tilted though thunder
Timelessly trampled, trapped, then teased   till the tiller toll the transcended triplets too...

This titan took terrible texture to
The technique tap tragically touching the tearful talent
Thereof tattooed tendons thoughtfully threatening thy tranced twilight
Theatrical the thought thumbing terror tightly they think

Tweet twice traumatized   talking tyrants taking trouble to torture totality
Therein teeters the trifecta
These tainted teal talismans telepathically tailgating the triforce tailored tome
Theologic to the torrent truth   that toxic tips transfixed tulips typical trifling thorns

RENÉE VERONA

...Tyrael!
Triumphantly tame thou throne to transmute treason,
Tarnishing the talons trademarked tenderly thereupon those thieves...

"Aurora Borealis" words that raged from the angel's lips
A spell to scorch the high heavens granting man enlightenment as the firmament was severed

Beware my foe

Onto a geosphere streets plated with gold
Flooded the atmosphere with divinity denying glory to the sun
Gaia moved throughout the cosmos heliocentric thus, to the universe a new star has been born

Blessings for Excalibur is a saber no more

My amour gilt like the stone, a paladin restored... Look for me among light
I will be there smiting demons as they still roam

Oh, Gungnir may you be gripped in woes...
Hear the here of my crusade dine between dusk and dawn either or our conflict will remain
Come stand before me villain, come and taste the fruits of defeat
That flourished from a tree of knowledge which you gave onto me

He came with haste striking with hell's fury grinding his vampiric teeth

We fought in time and belonging to time we ran rampantly
Him in his lust though, me in my vengeance, all to witness a tragedy
For he pieced my abdomen and I his heart...episodic both blows landed violently

Subdued I did not more the horror a nightmare as a sin today was I to bear?

Holy father forgive me as wrath took my spirit
Great lancer do not die, Great lancer do not fold
Save your life...change...become that which hold...

Sinister eyes gave way to a sinister smile a spear became that from a body turning cold
And in my fist, I grip a fallen foe as I pledged to reforge his lost soul

Yet, a fool I was again Lucifer's aura corrupted my consciousness
Moreover, a legion branded bad sat in my ill-fated mind including Gungnir with that dire smile

My will is no longer mine genocide reigned from the lance that made its home my palms
Killing man, angels, and demons all hail the beast untamed
A psychotic seraphic servant of the lord I claim

But who do I dare ask is my lord while I weeped in pain?

THE NIGHT SKY

Oblivion find this leviathan that plagues my perception
For I have drifted to the edges of my sanity
Lost in obscurity thirty days and thirty nights   with mayhem, chaos, to follow

The anarchy proclaimed as Satan's revolution

You desecrate a holy temple of God you foul swine s
Where the almighty is love benign art thou true love mine
If only I could conquer my own wits
Wasted pleas would not deafen my creator's ears not one bit

Fiendish along the halls infested in fury I gravitate
My sight leering darkness I felt like nothing more
Than a flea-bitten hell hound howling at the skies door

Be still the substances of this madness and, take a gaze

Radiant in her own sheen she came before me
The cherished gem I held for an eternity

The jewel that was dressed in a sapphire ocean blue dress
My eternal wife calypso the reason gold floods within my chest

A wave within infinity to bring calmness to any storm

Amidst this downpour when the waters turned against me
There was my goddess extending out her saving hands towards thee
Caressing my tear so that they could recede…

The hurricane which moved along my cerebral shadows
Took serenity as like a river flowing with harmony
Between the raindrops which liquefied her unforgettable kiss

Bliss…Oh, of wine my queen has always been so sweet…

A royal offset echoed this phrase to me
Make light this burden then, rise heaven's holy knight
For your eyes dye pure therefore, clean is thy soul king

Sing with me brothers hymns akin to redemption to repent
Bound parallel the moments where I stabbed her bosom with flit
After a realization that I was still a slave I decapitated the lady who made light concave

Bear witness Odin's eye that was gifted unto Mimir
A vile cutlass possessed blind an unholy sheer

RENÉE VERONA

Raving, wailing, and agonizing in disbelief
The sight of shear that transpired upon his beloved sheath
I vow to tear asunder this evil twisted abyss
The raven that thunders nevermore eradicating the soulless

I will be the horseman bring judgment day unto these wolves
Dog spewing dogma reckless fools   preaching how I became flawed as a claymore killing dragons
And, how slaying others became trademarked my fashion

My mind may have remained oh so clear
Yet, my bones soaked in everlasting sin when I pieced Gungnir

Still I lament the irony of it all…

Thusly, I took notice words the spearman grinned to say
My lesser a lesson in how to subdue, come with me enjoy the next act in our play

Excalibur the mercenary to excel death he entitled it
Where a story entails   a generation astray engulf in brimstone and madness
Having my face to be the image of the antichrist…One to lead the sleeping masses

Sadness, seeing silk satin sunsets sew such suffering
Nevertheless, adhere this that betides my fate
Forever falsified as a feeble forgery   counterfeited to clone the core crux that is corruption…

…The embodiment running towards chaos it seems…

Perceive crystals shining white with no value,   and pearly gates engraved yet gravely gem less
To comprehend my evanescent faith as I accepted my destiny…am I really, this helpless?

Is there any liberation for a humble creation I wondered…?

If so it may lie among the grounded fig leaves
The spectacle that sparked ionized particles to strike a fig tree
Discharging a stellar voice versifying the word "believe"

As two twin doves dove to aid a prisoner misguided
Landing upon my shoulders liberating my arms blessings to the almighty king of kings for sure

Please give me strength as I sever these lower ligaments

Thereby this demon crowded shell shall not move
Until I can bring about peace within thy own mind
For they do not need my consciousness to wield this body of mine
Thus, a finite journey to meditate absent to the ideals of time

THE NIGHT SKY

Transcend into the cerebellum I wish I had lobotomized
The nine circles internally fortified with Hades, himself as my unwanted guide
Followed the lawless renegade through the cold I did, haunted religiously by seven deadly sins

Brutes, rooted as the accused,   primed to take my existence if my torment no longer amused
So, I thought of white cherry blossoms to keep my composer
And in my thoughts among these demons did those blossoms bloom

Benevolent sacred petals swayed gently
As if a lullaby took chance to be their escort
What beauty I wondered   as I was being dressed within eve's looming shackles

Gungnir thus I murmured…   look…Can you see our salvation brother
It whispers from the mouth of these holy vines
Although he sneered at my words   I found glory with them
Moreover, in my mind the perception of my mind's eye

That which I lost in my hope for vengeance
That which I had forsaken within my quest for revenge

As did my kin Gungnir did

Not always was he so inked in bloodlust
For when I grabbed that moment to view these flowers did the truth of my enemy reveal itself

In a past life ages, and eons ago   he was the omnipotent spear of Odin
Never to miss his target therefore, he served in endless battles as the God's right hand

After a time that lasted beyond the scope of countless lives
Odin the wise granted him freedom…No longer did he, have to take that which was not his
No more did he, have to be a figure feared

Maybe he thought he could find a means to love
Lifetimes he searched and in a lifetime, he found one

She that was dressed in rubies   crowned of scarlet locks as to seduce a man's passion
Also in view a fire like crimson stare   that stood to sparked a flame within our hearts
A desire intensified to match that of the sun

Together would they have laughed in the summer running across a field of red roses
Singing with the cardinal fowls that flew by blessing their affection for one another
The earth too screamed praises to honor their joy
As volcanos erupted…echoing Krakatoa's perceptional vows

Heaven to them was like an inferno twisting with all the outstanding colors of time
They even had a child born to Arian blood ergo   on his birthday meteors fell with a blaze
To announce his forthcoming – Vulcan was his name

RENÉE VERONA

Yet, being of fire things tend to burn away
War came swift   and a nearby kingdom asked dear Gungnir for aid
To protect his family, he agreed to protect the kingdom
Although, never to step further than a journey's day

Malice...The king of Arcadia was a greedy man who hated not getting what he so wants

Therefore, on one war torn night Gungnir took post some ways from his home
And in the eve of night the king slaughtered his house hold
Thinking Gungnir to have no other attachments   except to the king's army's stronghold;
A fool the king's rightful color...plated gold

Gungnir raged at the sight of his dead beloved wife and son
His eyes cried with tears covered in blood that which his spear craved so much
He stormed the castle dethroning the royal family
Untamed like a wild beast and in the king's, last words... Mercy is what he pleaded

...Never have I seen a such suffering brought to a king...

Still Gungnir   lost to his insanity traveled home to burn his past
Though among the heart-breaking memories a letter lied last

A message that was written by his late wife;   A poem that spoke of his smile
Likewise did the sonnet state that if she should ever die
That his grin would be the only paradise need in her afterlife

Among these flowers my dear brother is our salvation I reiterated...

As "Aurora Borealis" echoed from my lips
My mind peered beyond the darkness scorching the high heaven's bliss
To awaken the heart of Gungnir out of that slumbering abyss

Therein a righteous flame appeared a woman of this a dress scarlet with ruby like diamonds
Sunna the sun, a star known as an ember's wish
The goddess draped in red murmured these words with a kiss to the spearman's cheek
Come with me our son waits for his father   the great Gungnir who loved me

Anger only grew upon the demonic lancer's face
Peering down everyone with malice, chalice for it may be my last drink

Fear stood over all..." Tectonic Tranny" the words that growled through his teeth

A loud tremor coursed through the depths of my mind, thus his sorcery relieving those imps from me
Yet, because of my lacerated legs I was unable to move
Though when I blinked   Gungnir had already started killing the devilish fools

THE NIGHT SKY

His wife the phoenix of heaven healed my wounds
Begging in tears that I stop his spear and the gore attuned
So, I summoned seven forbidden swords from the sky
To pin a warrior who for years was mortified

In return for seven eons would I be unconscious to time

Lucifer fled leaving behind the phrase wasn't it all so sublime
...Glory...Divine... Tyrael appeared "Awaken" he shouted then all became clear...

This was a dream as I awoke in the haven of my chambers

With my love standing at my side as lovely as the ocean blue teal tide
Together, Tyrael stood there to clarify
Looking deeply into the fragmented pieces of my mind

You are the chosen prophet cursed with the gift to foresee
Gungnir will come make sure you are ready
For devils also have those that are haunted by prophecy
The sword and the spear are forever tied through the fate of destiny.